Charles M. Kurtz

Illustrationsfrom the Art gallery of the World's Columbian

exposition

Charles M. Kurtz

Illustrationsfrom the Art gallery of the World's Columbian exposition

ISBN/EAN: 9783741162732

Manufactured in Europe, USA, Canada, Australia, Japa

Cover: Foto ©Thomas Meinert / pixelio.de

Manufactured and distributed by brebook publishing software
(www.brebook.com)

Charles M. Kurtz

Illustrationsfrom the Art gallery of the World's Columbian

exposition

THE

WORLD'S COLUMBIAN EXPOSITION

THE ART GALLERY

WEST PAVILION

SOUTH COURT

WEST COURT

ROTUNDA

NORTH COURT

EAST COURT

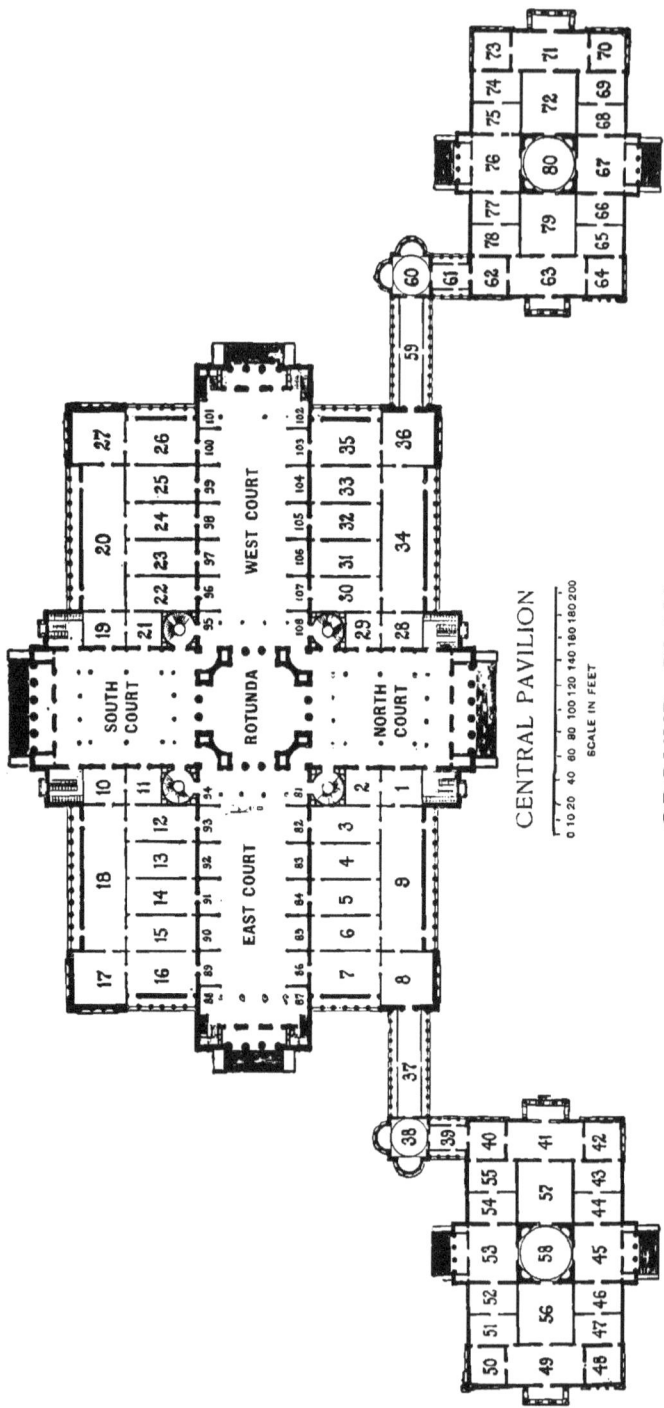

CENTRAL PAVILION

0 10 20 40 60 80 100 120 140 160 180 200
SCALE IN FEET

GROUND PLAN

EAST PAVILION

PLAN OF UPPER GALLERY

CENTRAL PAVILION

SOUTH COURT — **WEST COURT** — **ROTUNDA** — **NORTH COURT** — **EAST COURT**

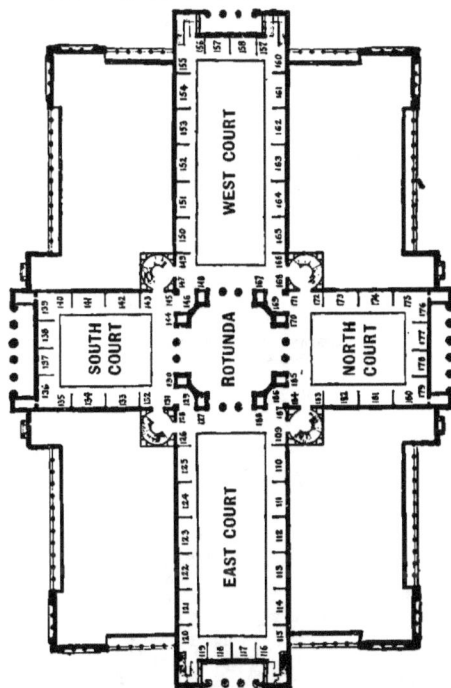

OFFICIAL

ILLUSTRATIONS

(THREE HUNDRED AND THIRTY-SIX ENGRAVINGS)

FROM THE

ART GALLERY

OF THE

WORLD'S COLUMBIAN EXPOSITION

EDITED BY

CHARLES M. KURTZ

ASSISTANT CHIEF OF THE ART DEPARTMENT
WORLD'S COLUMBIAN EXPOSITION

FIRST EDITION

GEORGE BARRIE, PHILADELPHIA

EXCLUSIVE PUBLISHER OF ALL OFFICIAL ILLUSTRATED PUBLICATIONS RELATING
TO THE DEPARTMENTS OF FINE AND LIBERAL ARTS

CENTRAL PAVILION OF THE ART PALACE

INTRODUCTORY

This book, illustrating many of the most important paintings and sculptures selected for exhibition in the Art Department of the World's Columbian Exposition,—an exposition greater in plan, scope, and achievement than any other that has been undertaken in the whole history of the world,—is prepared for two classes of persons—those who visit the Exposition and those who may not be so fortunate.

To those who visit the Exposition, it aims to be, in some sense, a preparation and a guide. It points out works especially worthy of attention and study among the hundreds of masterpieces by the leading artists of the various countries of the world; it designates the sections and galleries where these particular works may be found; it gives a complete, numbered plan of the galleries of the Art Palace, showing the sections respectively occupied by the different nations (so that one may find one's way among them with the greatest ease) and, lastly, it presents data concerning the artists whose works are illustrated,—data which, though necessarily brief, is extremely valuable in usually affording clue to the origin of special characteristics shown in the technique of their works, thus often aiding one better to understand and appreciate them.

7

After the Exposition is over, and its magnificent display of art has become only an influence and a memory, the illustrations herein given will serve to freshen fading recollections and will bring back to the mind a measure of the splendors of the great event for which the year 1893—indeed, the nineteenth century itself—promises to be especially noted.

To those who may not visit the Exposition, the illustrations of the art exhibits will convey an idea of them that could be obtained in no other manner so effective or adequate. Being engraved directly from photographs of the works, the illustrations are absolutely accurate in detail. They lack only size and color.

Through this publication, prepared with the sanction and under the direct supervision of the Art Department, it is the aim to stimulate interest in art and to assist those desiring to take advantage of the great opportunity which the art exhibit offers for study. It is hoped that the book may find appreciation not only in the present, but that, in future, it may be esteemed precious as a souvenir and valuable as a record.

*   *   *   *   *

Primarily, the object of an exposition may be assumed to be educational. By bringing together productions of various classes from all portions of the globe opportunity is afforded for study and comparison. Each exhibitor may learn something from almost every other exhibitor in his class which may be to his advantage, and which may lead to the improvement of that which he produces, whether it be in the domain of art or manufacture. At the same time, the general visitor to the Exposition likewise may gain new ideas, and correct impressions that have been formed upon insufficient or erroneous data.

The measure of the value of an exposition is determined by the number of important countries represented by exhibits, the characteristic and comprehensive nature of these exhibits, and their excellence in quality, according to the standards of the countries from which they come.

These considerations were kept constantly in mind by the authorities of the Art Department of the World's Columbian Exposition. The Chief of the Art Department, Professor Halsey C. Ives, after formulating plans for the organization of the American Section, visited France, England, Germany, Holland, Belgium, Norway, Sweden, Denmark, Russia, Poland, Austria, Austro-Hungary, Italy, and Spain, where he conferred with prominent government officials, leading artists, the heads of the great art museums, academies, and schools, noted collectors of art works, and others, with the aim of creating such interest in the Exposition and its Art Department that characteristic and excellent exhibits might be secured from all these countries. In every case it was urged that the exhibit be made from the standpoint of quality rather than quantity, and this consideration found favor with the various foreign commissioners.

As a result of Professor Ives's visits abroad, applications for space in the Art Department were made by every country which had been visited. These applications, in almost every case, called for amounts of space far exceeding what it was possible to assign. Indeed, from foreign governments alone, the applications for wall-space aggregated nearly 300,000 square feet. The total wall-space of the Art Gallery is about 200,000 square feet. After reserving 35,000 square feet for the American Section, there remained about 165,000 square feet to be distributed among all the foreign countries applying for space. And this is not a small amount; it is more than double the space that was occupied by foreign countries in the Art Department of the Centennial Exhibition, held in Philadelphia in 1876.

The countries that are represented officially in the Art Department of the World's Columbian Exposition are France, Germany, Great Britain, Austria, Spain, Italy, Belgium, Holland, Norway,

Sweden, Denmark, Russia, Canada, Mexico, and Japan. The largest amount of space assigned to any country has been reserved for the United States; and next in order come France, Germany, Great Britain, Italy, Belgium, and Austria. France receives 29,200 square feet. The smallest assignment has been made to Mexico,—one of the few countries receiving all the space asked for,—1500 square feet.

As nearly every country's assignment of space is so far less than the amount asked for, the result was, as might have been expected, the exercise of greater discrimination in the selection of exhibits than otherwise might have seemed warranted, and this has been really of very great advantage to the art exhibit as a whole; the standard of excellence thereby being raised much higher than usually has obtained in international exhibitions.

Undoubtedly there is at this Exposition a better general representation of the world's art than has been made at any exposition in the past. Excellent, in the main, as have been the French expositions, they have very slightly represented German art, and, on the other hand, the German expositions have contained little or no French art. Russian art has been seen very little outside of Russia, and the Scandinavian artists have not received adequate attention in the great expositions of the past. English art was largely represented at the Centennial Exhibition, but the selection of the works shown was not made with anything like the degree of discrimination exercised in the choice of works for the British Section in the World's Columbian Exposition.

The selection of exhibits from the various foreign countries in most cases was made by committees of artists, working under the jurisdiction of Art Commissioners appointed by the government of the country. In France, M. Antonin Proust was made the Art Commissioner—a most excellent appointment. M. Proust, it will be remembered, was the Director of the Art Department of the French International Exposition of 1889. He was Minister of

Arts in the Gambetta Cabinet, and is widely recognized as one of the highest authorities on French art—both of the past and the present. After having thoroughly organized the French art exhibit —in which work he was most ably assisted by M. A.-Barthélemy,— M. Proust resigned, and M. Roger Ballu was then appointed Commissioner. M. Ballu had been editor of *l'Art*, was President and had been one of the founders of the French Society of Pastellists, etc. M. Ballu took up the work where M. Proust laid it down, and admirably carried it to completion. In this he was efficiently assisted by M. Henri Giudicelli, who came to instal the exhibits.

Mr. H. W. Mesdag, famous as an artist and as one of the most enlightened art collectors in Europe, was appointed Art Commissioner for the Netherlands. Mr. Mesdag supervised the formation of the Dutch exhibit, while Mr. Hubert Vos, the distinguished painter, was placed in charge of affairs as Acting Commissioner in this country. In Great Britain, the interests of the Art Section were committed to the Royal Society of Arts, which appointed a committee to look after the collection of an exhibit. Of this committee, Sir Frederick Leighton, President of the Royal Academy, was made the head. Herr Schnars-Alquist, noted as a marine painter, wisely was selected by his government to organize the German art exhibit. Professor Ernest Slingeneyer, the historical painter, was placed in charge of Belgian art interests. Signor Giulio Monteverde, the sculptor, was made the president of the central committee for Italy. Later, Signor Angelo del Nero was appointed Commissioner of Fine Arts by his government, and to his efficient services the Italian art exhibit mainly is due. Mr. Anders Zorn, one of the most celebrated painters of his country, was appointed Commissioner of Fine Arts for Sweden, and admirably has served his country in this capacity. All these gentlemen entered upon their respective tasks with a degree of enthusiasm that soon was communicated to the artists, and led to the bringing forward of the best work obtainable from all quarters. The care with which selections were made from the almost innumerable productions offered is attested by the exhibits in the various foreign sections. In this connection, mention must be made of the very valuable service which Mr. S. Tegima, of Japan, rendered his government—as well as the Exposition—in organizing and installing the remarkable Japanese exhibit. Never before this time has Japan been represented in the Art Department of an International Exposition; but never before has the country been given such an opportunity. Recognizing the radical differences between Japanese art and that of the western world, the authorities of the Art Department of the Columbian Exposition did not bind Japanese art exhibitors to the rigid classification established for other nations, but urged that the exhibit be made thoroughly national in character— exactly such an exhibit as would be formed under a classification devised for an art exhibition to be held in Japan. Mr. Tegima, appreciating this opportunity, embraced and has made the most of it.

The foreign artists had a powerful incentive to send their best works to America aside from their disposition to do everything possible to enhance the credit of their respective countries in art production. During the past few years they have seen the United States become one of the greatest markets for art works in the world. They have noted the stupendous prices that have been paid by our millionaire collectors for famous pictures in the public sales in Paris, London, and New York, and they have observed the steady stream of art productions of the highest excellence—both ancient and modern —coming from France, Holland, Germany, and England. Every foreign artist, therefore, appreciated the value of the reputation he might gain by an exhibit of especially noteworthy productions.

The American artists likewise had an incentive to make the best possible exhibit; here was the great opportunity to show that the works of American artists could stand comparison with the productions of the artists of the other nations. With the endeavor of securing the best possible exhibit of American art, the Exposition authorities, at the instance of the Chief of the Art Department, appointed Advisory Committees—consisting of painters, sculptors, architects, engravers, and the followers of other branches of art— to look after the interests of American artists in those sections of this country and Europe which were considered especial centres of American art activity. Such committees were established in New York, Philadelphia, Boston, Paris, Munich, London, Rome, and Florence, and their membership comprised many of the ablest and most distinguished artists this country has produced.

When the time arrived for the selection of works to be exhibited in Chicago, the various Advisory Committees were constituted juries by a system involving an interchange of service amongst the members of different committees, thus securing to each jury a national rather than a strictly local character. Artists residing in the central, western, southern, and extreme northern portions of the United States had the privilege of submitting their works to a national jury in Chicago. This jury was composed of artists chosen from different sections of the country.

In order to secure a retrospective exhibit of American art, a special committee was appointed, having representatives in New York, Philadelphia, and Boston; this committee solicited from public institutions and private owners such works as its members believed best would represent the historical development of art in America. This exhibit is exceedingly interesting. It includes notable works by American painters who were famous in their day, and justly so, but who, in later times, are almost forgotten—owing to the fact that general art-interest has been absorbed by work of more modern methods, though often of less truly artistic character.

The interesting exhibit of noteworthy foreign paintings belonging to American collections was formed through the kindness. of prominent picture owners, from whom they were specially solicited.

One of the most noteworthy exhibits in the Art Department is the collection of casts duplicating reproductions of monumental works shown in the Museum of Comparative Sculpture in the Palace of the Trocadero, Paris. These casts not only illustrate the history of French sculpture, but also the development of architecture as a fine art in France during mediæval and later times. They comprise examples of the Romanesque, Gothic, Renaissance, and some of the more modern work. Some of the casts, reproducing large portions of the façades of cathedrals, churches, monasteries, and other important structures are of very considerable size and of remarkable elaboration in detail. A portion of this collection (casts to the value of over 50,000 francs) generously was presented to the Exposition by the French Government, upon the condition that, at the close of the Exposition, these casts should become the property of an American Art Museum.

The Art Gallery is one of the most beautiful of all the Exposition structures. The architecture is Ionic of the most refined type, the order being taken from the Erechtheum of the Acropolis at Athens. The galleries and courts for the exhibition of paintings and sculptures are of varying proportions, are lighted from above, and the structure is fire-proof. The three great sections—the Central, East, and West Pavilions—aggregate, in extreme length, 1152 feet, and in depth 504 feet. The main walls are of brick, covered with "staff," a composition of plaster-of-Paris and other ingredients, which has, when finished, the appearance of stone. The roof is of iron, steel, and glass, and all columns, staircases, etc., are of iron. There are eighty galleries, ranging in size from 30 feet square to 36 by 120 feet, for the exhibition of paintings, besides one hundred and eight alcoves, fronting upon the courts of the Central Pavilion —twenty-eight on the first floor and eighty on the second—giving additional wall-space. There are four large courts and a rotunda in the Central Pavilion, and a rotunda in each of the other pavilions for the exhibition of sculptures and architectural works. From the exterior architectural standpoint, the Art Palace justly may be considered one of the chief of the art exhibits.

THE ART GALLERY, ILLUSTRATED

WITH

THREE HUNDRED AND THIRTY-SIX
ENGRAVINGS

IVAN TVOROZHNIKOV (Russia)   A LAY BROTHER: IMAGE SELLER

EUG. VAIL (United States)   MARINE

V. E. DEMONT-BRETON   A YOUNG SAILOR'S TRAINING

ADOLPH BINET (France)   THE LOVERS

P. JOLYET (France)   MIGNON

FRANK S. HOLMAN (United States)   MELODY

A SIMPLE SONG

W. M. GAY (United States)

PASSING THE RING

A. BARTHOLOME (France)

FISHMONGER—DIEPPE

DOMINIQUE ROZIER (France)

VENICE

JULES L. STEWART (United States)

THE KNITTING SCHOOL

G. HENKES (Holland)

THE HORSE FAIR—ROTTERDAM

OTTO EERELMAN (Holland)

AUTUMN

Louis APOL. (Holland)

NOVEMBER SUNSHINE

WALTER NETTLETON (United States)

ALONE IN THE WORLD

JOSEF ISRAELS (Holland)

THE SHEPHERD AT HIS LUNCH

G. S. TRUESDELL (United States)

AN INNOCENT VICTIM

SEYMOUR THOMAS (United States)

EVENING

Louis P. DESSAR (United States)

FOR ANCHOR

H. W. MESDAG (Holland)

MINERS ON STRIKE

G. LA TOUCHE (France)

THE VALLEY OF THE SEVILLO

LEON BARILLOT (France)

TRAIN 47

L. BARILLOT (France)

A FAMILY

HENRY BONNEFOY (France)

THE OUTPOSTS

W. VELTEN (Germany)

EXPECTING RETURN OF THE BOATS

ELCHANON VERVEER (Holland)

SURF

HANS VON BARTELS (Germany)

THE BRICKYARD

WALTER LEISTIKOW (Germany)

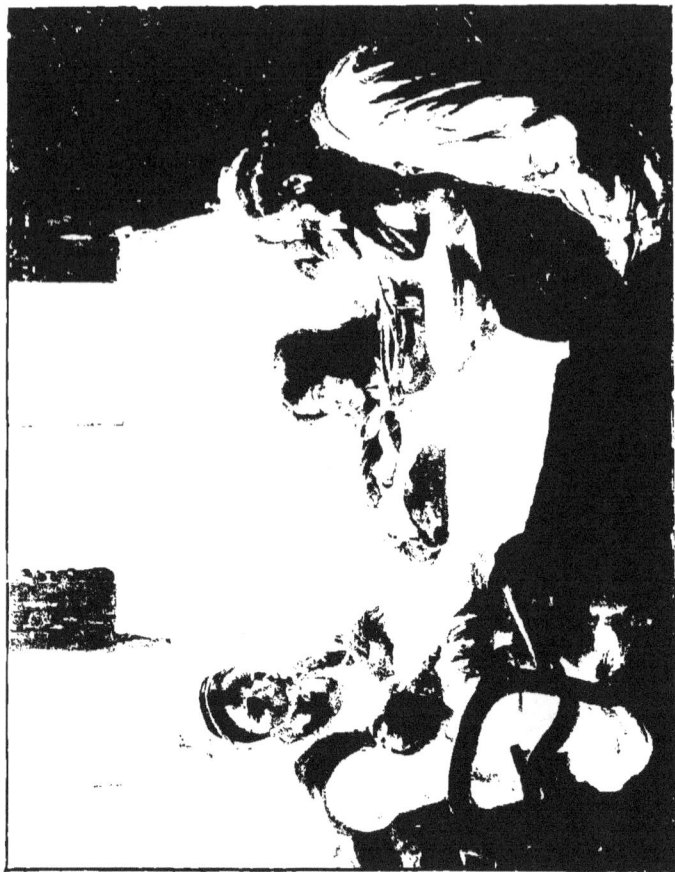

THE FAMILY MEAL

ELIZABETH NOURSE (United States)

NORMAN BULL

W. H. HOWE (United States)

REDEMPTION OF TANNHÄUSER

FRANK DICKSEE (Great Britain)

A SOBER MEAL

ALBERT NEUHUYS (Holland)

A STORM AT YPORT

EUGÈNE BERTHELON (France)

AN INN IN OLD COTILLE

F. DE VUILLEFROY (France)

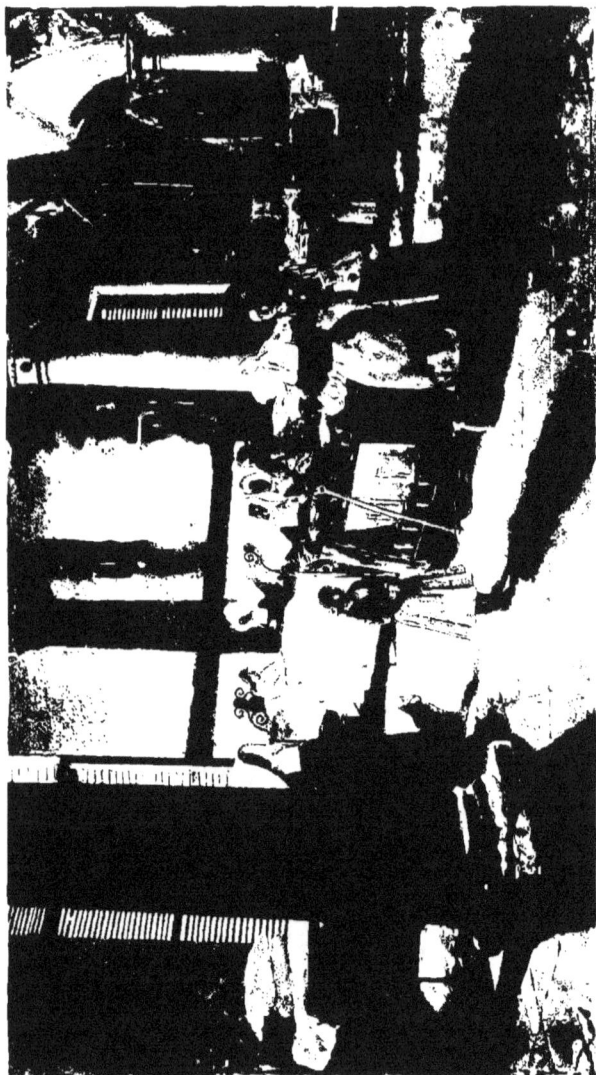

SISTERS OF CHARITY

J. AGRASOT Y JUAN (Spain)

BAY OF SAN MICHEL

ALEXANDER NOZAL. (France)

ON THE NILE AT BENI HASSEN

PROSPER L. SENAT (United States)

A COUNTRY VILLA

E. PETITJEAN (France)

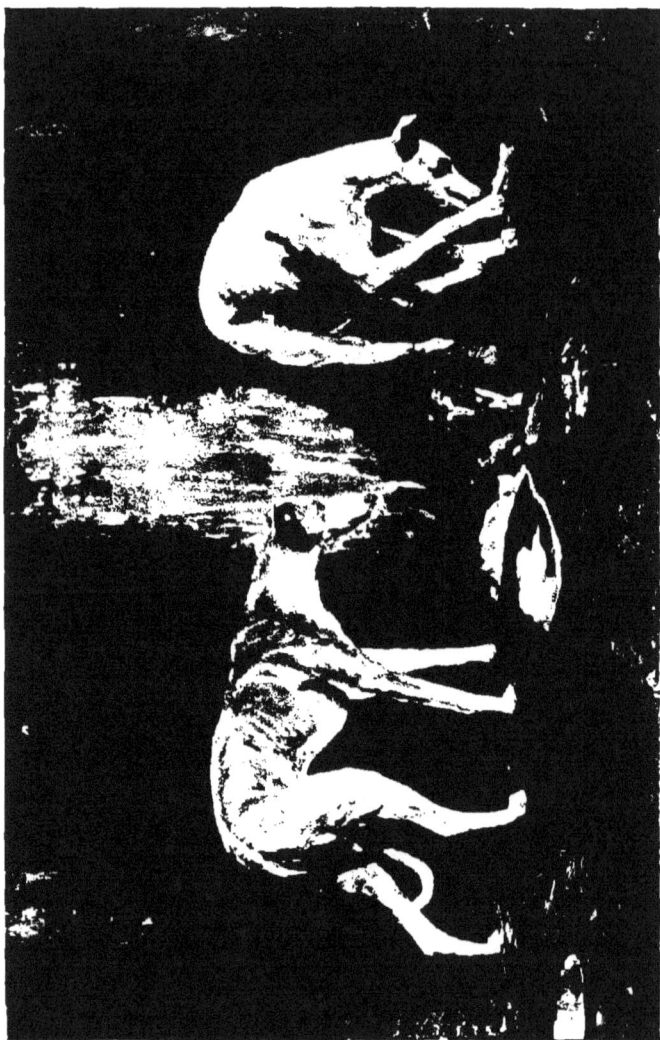

IDA VON SCHÜCHSENHEIM (Sweden)

A SUDDEN ATTACK

JOSEPH VON BRANDT (Germany)

DONKEYS ON THE SHORE—PICARDY

J. H. DE HAAS (Holland)

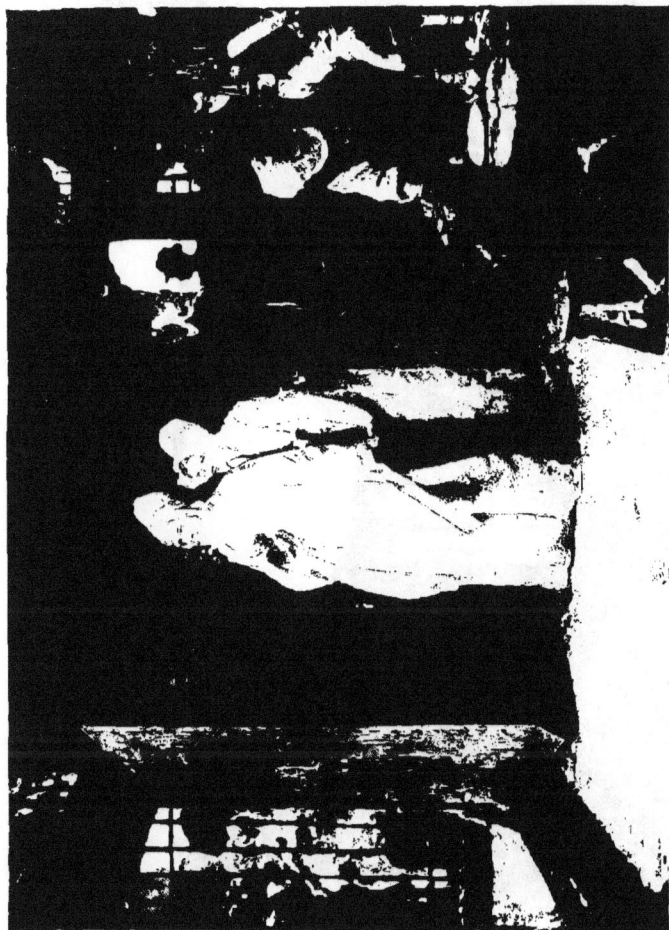

MRS. E. M. WARD (Great Britain)

MRS. FRY VISITING NEWGATE

EDOUARD TOUDOUZE (France)   THE CRADLE

G. PAULI (Sweden)   MIDSUMMER'S NIGHT

11. TEMPLE (Austria)   PORTRAIT OF W. UNGER

CARL GUTHERZ (United States) THE ANGEL ON THE GRAVE

A. DAWANT (France)   THE END OF THE MASS

J. J. TVOROJUIKOF (Russia) GRANDMOTHER AND GRAND-DAUGHTER

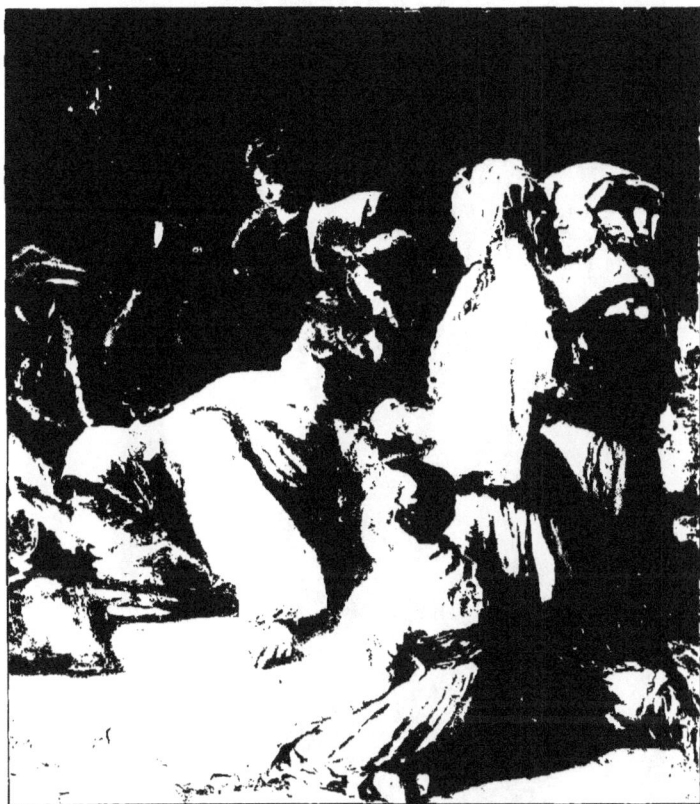

ELIZABETH NOURSE (United States)   GOOD FRIDAY

PAUL SINIBALDI (France)   THE DAUGHTER OF THE
RAJAHS

M. VILLEGAS-VRIEVA (Spain)   REMEMBRANCES

G. HENKES (Holland)   A DUTCH PEASANT

WALTER M. GAY (United States)   MASS IN BRITTANY

Madeleine LEMAIRE (France)   FALL OF THE LEAVES

W. H. Y. TITCOMB (Great Britain)   PRIMITIVE METHODISTS AT
ST. IVES, CORNWALL

AD. BRÜTT (Germany)   PHRYNE

AD. BRÜTT (Germany)   SAVED

W. T. DANNAT (United States)   SPANISH GIRL

Mrs. S. MESDAG-VAN HOUTEN (Holland)   COTTAGE

A. BOMPIANI (Italy)   IN THE WOODS

G. GUARDA-CASSI (Italy)   THE MAYOR'S WEDDING

ALF. AGACHE (France)   THE ANNUNCIATION

A. GUERRA (Italy)   CIOCARA WITH FLOWERS

CHAS. GRAFLY (United States)   DÆDALUS

J. B. KNIGHT (Great Britain)   HADLEY CHURCH, NEAR BARNET

EDWARD A. BELL (United States)   PORTRAIT IN GRAY

SURPRISED

E. J. BOKS (Holland)

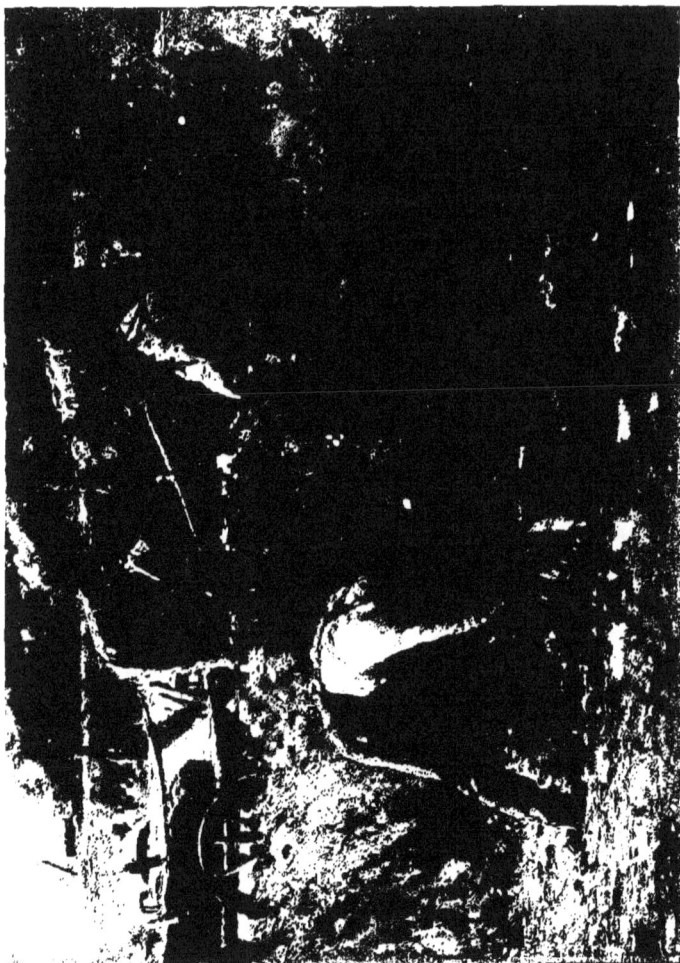

SOUTH DUXBURY CLAM-DIGGER

JOHN J. ENNEKING (United States)

THE END OF A ROMANCE

EVARISTE-VITAL LUMINAIS (France)

LAKE IN THE APENNINES

Pietro BARUCCI (Italy)

LUNCH ON THE GRASS

M. REALIER-DUMAS (France)

NIGHT, SWEDISH COAST

ALF. WAHLBERG (Sweden)

WASHING-DAY

B. J. BLOMMERS (Holland)

GLAD SPRING

GEO. WETHERBEE (Great Britain)

THE WHEAT-SHEAVES

F. J. QUIGNON (France)

THE WHITE SAIL

N. BASTERT (Holland)

LEGEND OF THE DESERT

F. MELL DE MOND (United States)

FLOWER CULTURE IN THE NEIGHBORHOOD OF NICE

E. DAMERON (France)

GLEANERS

ALESSANDRO BATTAGLIA (Italy)

VICTORY OF FAITH

Sr. GEORGE HARE (Great Britain)

FARM-HOUSE IN LIMBURG

W. C. NUKKEN (Holland)

LAKESIDE

W. M. CHASE (United States)

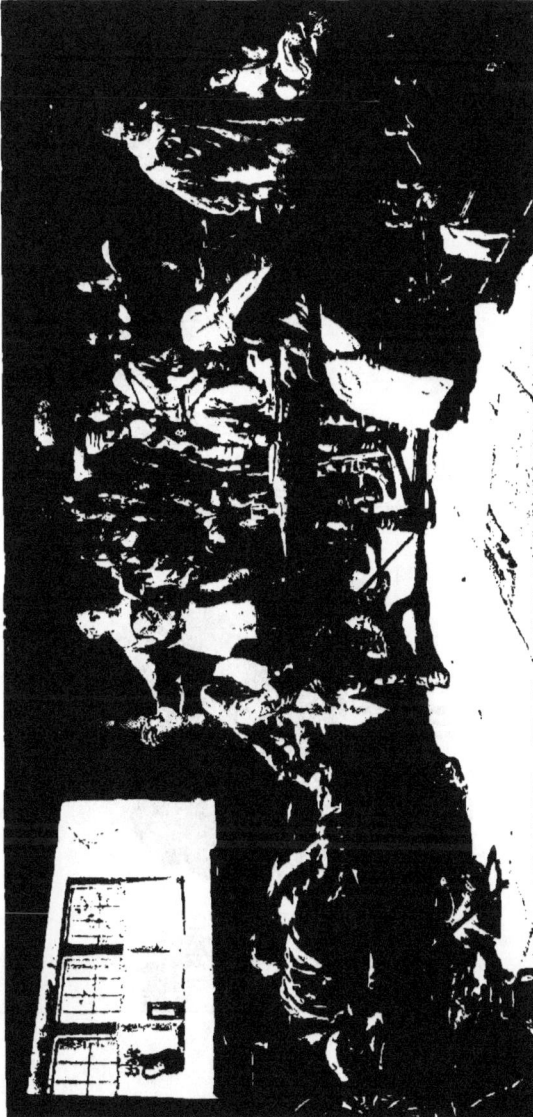

THE CAPTAIN OF THE TROOP

F. DADD (Great Britain)

CHARLES-EDOUARD DELORT (France)

CAPTURE OF THE DUTCH FLEET IN THE TEXEL BY THE HUSSARS OF THE REPUBLIC, 1793

INTERIOR OF COW-HOUSE

OSCAR BJORCK (Sweden)

WRECK OF THE SPANISH ARMADA

F. WALTON (Great Britain)

THREE BEGGARS OF CORDOVA

E. LORD WEEKS (United States)

SAILORS PLAYING CARDS

H. S. TUKE (Great Britain)

HARVEST-TIME

G. G. MIASOIEDOFF (Russia)

THE CONFERENCE

JOSEF MUNSCH (Germany)

J. EMILE SAINTIN (France)   REVERIE

CHAS. SPRAGUE PEARCE (United States) MADAM P . . .

AUGUSTE GLAIZE (France) THE BLIND MAN AND THE
PARALYTIC

L. C. TIFFANY (United States)   TAMING THE FLAMINGO

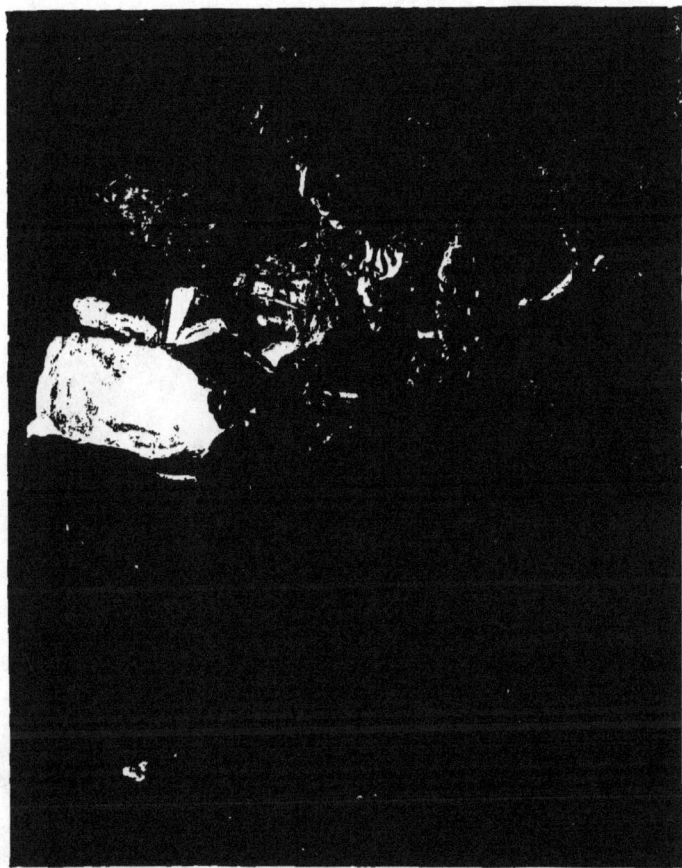

ADOLF HOELZEL (Germany)   LIGHT

W. MARTENS (Holland)   AT THE WELL

G. L. BULLEID (Great Britain)   AT THE TEMPLE GATE

J. F. RAFFAELLI (France)   THE GRANDFATHER

FRED MAX BREDT (Germany)   TWO GAZELLES

Publio De TOMMASI (Italy)   GAME OF CHESS—IN THE
VATICAN

C. E. PERUGINI (Great Britain)   A SUMMER SHOWER

J. A. MUENIER (France)   WOMEN OF ALGERIA

JAMES CHARLES (Great Britain)   IN MEMORY OF · . . .

N. KOUZNETZOFF (Russia)   IN THE GARDEN

F. A. DELOBBE (France)   A BITE AFTER THE BATH

JOHN R. REID (Great Britain)   THE YARN

THE MAIDENS' RACE

J. R. WEGUELIN (Great Britain)

THE SHEPHERDESS

CHAS. SPRAGUE PEARCE (United States)

THE CURSE OF THE FAMILY

T. B. KENNINGTON (Great Britain)

AT BREAKFAST

NICHOLAS SAGORSKI (Russia)

POMOSA

GEO. W. MAYNARD (United States)

NAPLES

R. SANTORO (Italy)

RUDOLPH PHRENZ (Russia)

A. APOLLONI (Italy)   BEATRICE

AFTERNOON IN THE MEADOWS

H. S. BISBING (United States)

THE HERRING SEASON

FRANK C. PENFOLD (United States)

PÆSTUM

F. CORTESE (Italy)

SINGING-LESSON IN A COMMON-SCHOOL IN PARIS

A. TRUPHEME (France)

ALEXIS KIWCHENKO (Russia)

AT THE CRATERS OF LENDJI, NEAR JERUSALEM

IN A VILLA AT EL BIAR, ALGIERS

F. A. BRIDGMAN (United States)

ON THE RIVER BANK

H. S. BISBING (United States)

CAVALIER, PERIOD OF LOUIS XIII

THOS. W. SHIELDS (United States)

DEPARTURE OF THE FLEET

WALTER LANGLEY (Great Britain)

INTEMPERANCE

T. E. DUVERGER (France)

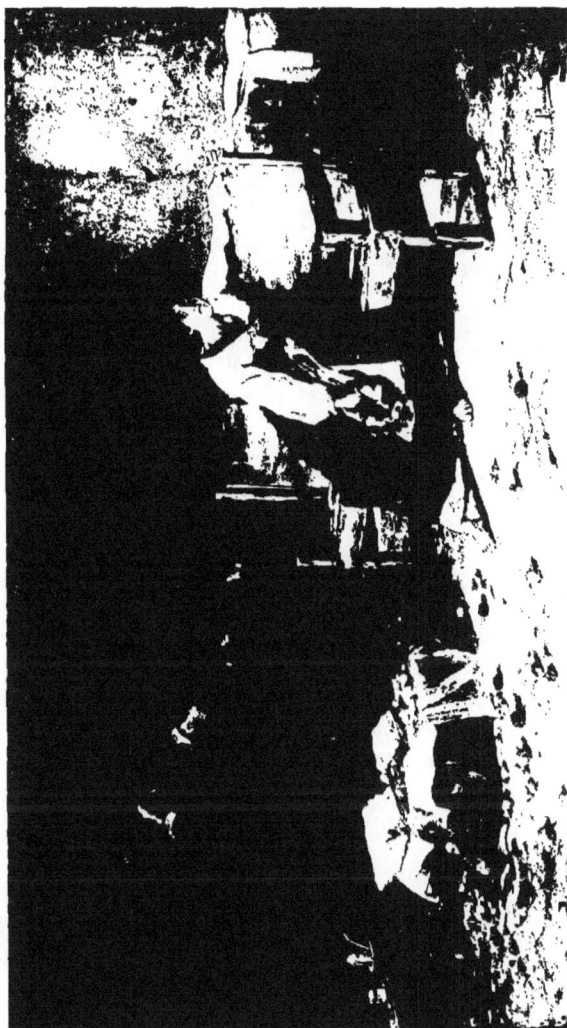

CRAZY

Domenico PENNACCHINI (Italy)

SEALING THE LETTER

CHAS. CURRAN (United States)

CHRIST AT THE HOUSE OF MARY AND MARTHA

H. SIEMIRADSKI (Russia)

EXCAVATIONS IN ROME

PAUL KOVALEVSKI (Russia)

PLOUGHING, SPRING

H. J. VAN DER WELLE (Holland)

GULF OF AJACCIO, CORSICA

PROSPER L. SENAT (United States)

THE GANGES

E. LORD WEEKS

FLOWER GATHERING IN THE SOUTH OF FRANCE

W. LOGSDAIL (Great Britain)

COW RESTING

Jan VROLŸK (Holland)

THE SUNSHINE OF LIFE

J. A. MUENIER (France)

YOUTH

ADRIEN-LOUIS DEMONT (France)

PLEASURES OF THE PAST

A. B. SEWELL. (United States)

ALBERT MAIGNAN (France)   DEATH OF WILLIAM THE CONQUEROR

SORTING FEATHERS

A. KIWCHENKO (Russia)

SYLVAN FESTIVAL

A. B. SEWELL (United States)

G. COURTOIS (France)   PORTRAIT OF MME. GAUTREAU

FRED. HALL (Great Britain)   RESULT OF HIGH LIVING

A. CHEVALIER TAYLER (Great Britain)   THE PEDDLER

A. B. SEWELL (United States)   MOTHER AND SON

G. MOREAU DE TOURS (France)   CARNOT AT WATTIGNIES

ALBERT NEUHUYS (Holland)   MOTHER'S DELIGHT

ALFRED-PIERRE AGACHE (France)   VANITY

Max BAUMBACH (Germany)   DANCING FIGURES

MARIE S. LUCAS (Great Britain)   HENRY VI

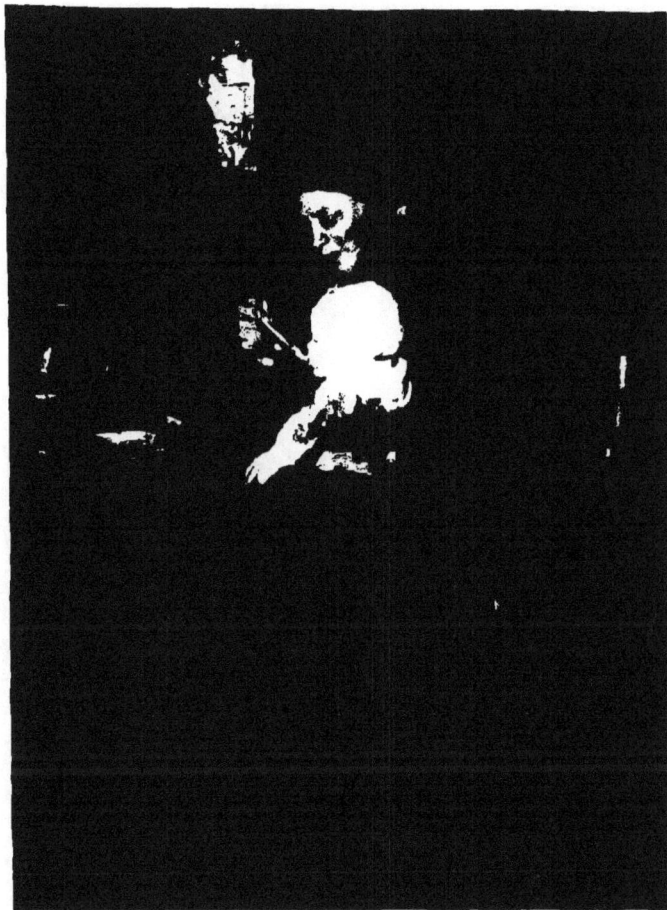

ALBERT NEUHUYS (Holland)   DUTCH WOMAN AND CHILD

T. A. PELEVIN (Russia)   THE FIRST BORN

OLD GATE OF THE TIBER AT ROME

CAMILLE PARIS (France)

WEDDING DAY

E. L. HENRY (United States)

WINDMILL IN THE LOWLANDS

P. J. C. GAMBRIEL. (Holland)

A MOMENT'S REST

W. E. NORTON (United States)

LEON COUTURIER (France)

AT THE CAPSTAN—ALL TOGETHER

THE SCARLET LETTER

RHODA HOLMES NICHOLS (United States)

GOING FREELY

H. SCHNARS-ALQUIST (Germany)

OCTOBER TWILIGHT IN NEW ENGLAND

J. J. ENNEKING (United States)

THE SEINERS' RETURN

WALTER L. DEAN (United States)

LAWN-TENNIS PARTY

ORRIN S. PARSONS (United States)

A SANDY ROAD

F. P. TER MEUTEN (Holland)

THE TWO MILLS

JACOB MARIS (Holland)

EVICTED

B. FLETCHER (Great Britain)

ON THE ZUYDER ZEE—ISLE OF MARKEN

J. M. TEN KATE (Holland)

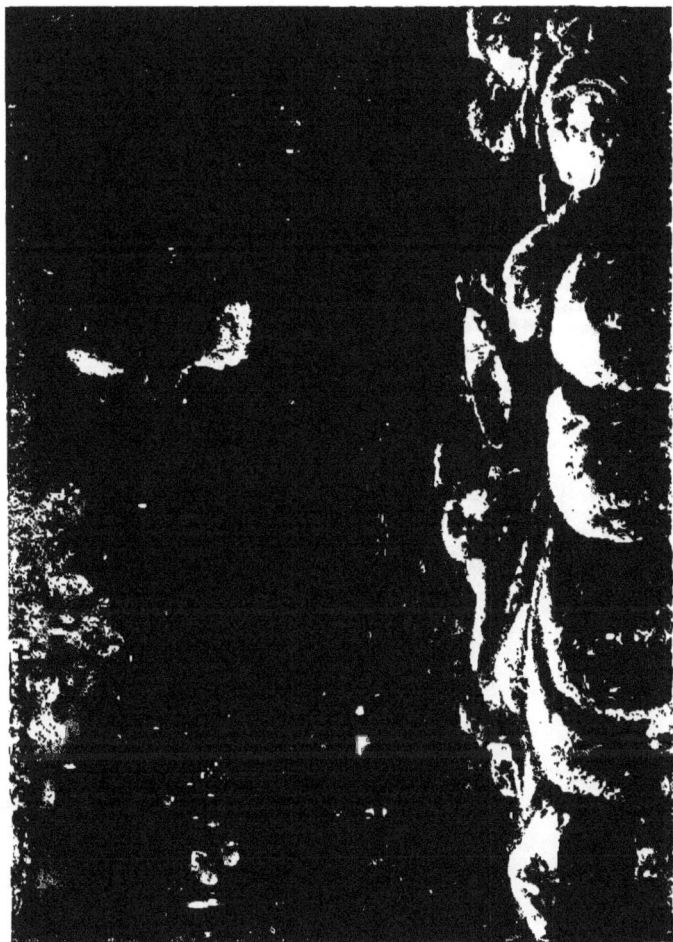

SALTING SHEEP

J. J. ENNEKING (United States)

EARLY SNOW

WALTER PALMER (United States)

AT ETAPLES, PAS DE CALAIS

EUGENE CHIGOT (France)

HUGO KÖNIG (Germany)

PAUL HOECKER (Germany)   ON BOARD H. M. S. "DEUTSCHLAND"

THE RETURN

A. MARAIS (France)

ON THE BEACH

C. M. McILHENNY (United States)

THE LAST BREATH

H. GUILLÉN PEDEMONTE (Spain)

FETE DIEU—DIEPPE, NORMANDY

PHIL. R. MORRIS (Great Britain)

W. E. NORTON (United States)   RETURN OF HERRING FLEET

WALTER MAC EWEN (United States) THE ABSENT ONE ON ALL SOULS' DAY

PAUL-ALEXANDER-ALFRED LEROY (France)   CHRIST HEALING THE BLIND

Josef GISELA (Austria)   THE LOTTERY

CHAS. SPRAGUE PEARCE (United States)   THE ANNUNCIATION

MAURICE BOMPARD (France)　　　　THE OLD CHELMA GATE

HERM. KAULBACH (Germany)   ONCE UPON A TIME

WALTER L. DEAN (United States)   THE OPEN SEA

BY THE RIVER

A. B. SEWELL (United States)

THE BROKEN IDOL

VAL. C. PRINSEP (Great Britain)

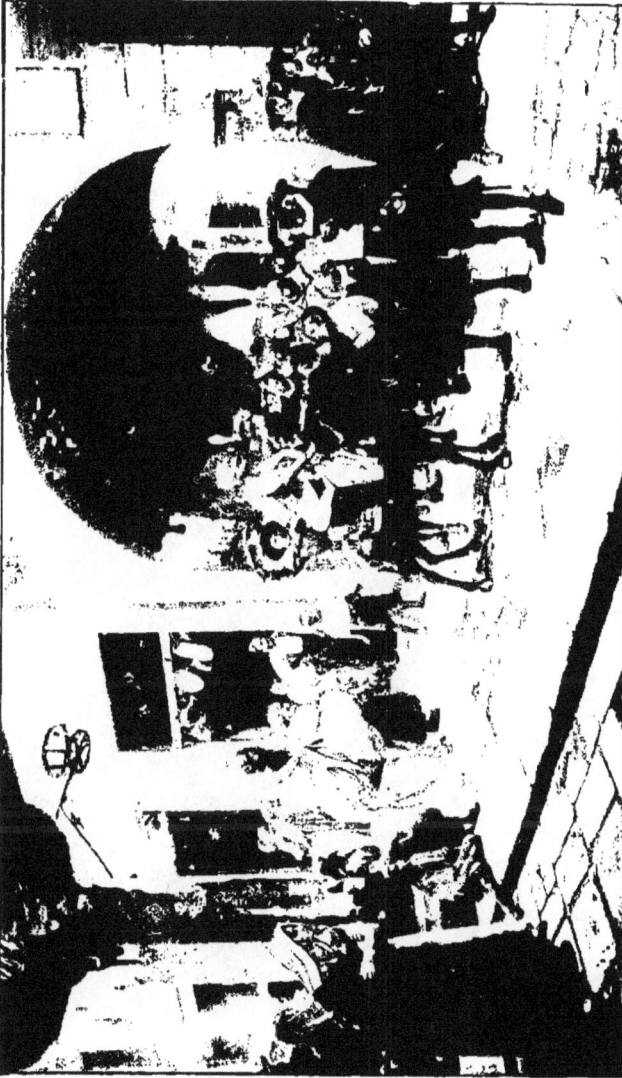

PUNISHMENT BY THE LASH

F. GALOFRE V OLLER (Spain)

BIRD SHOOTING

BRUNO LILJEFORS (Sweden)

ITALIAN IDYL

CHAS. ULRICH (United States)

A SUMMER NIGHT, VENICE

S. M. FISHER (Great Britain)

THERESE SCHWARTZE (Holland)   THE ORPHAN GIRLS, AMSTERDAM

HARVESTERS HOMEWARD BOUND

E. HENSELER (Germany)

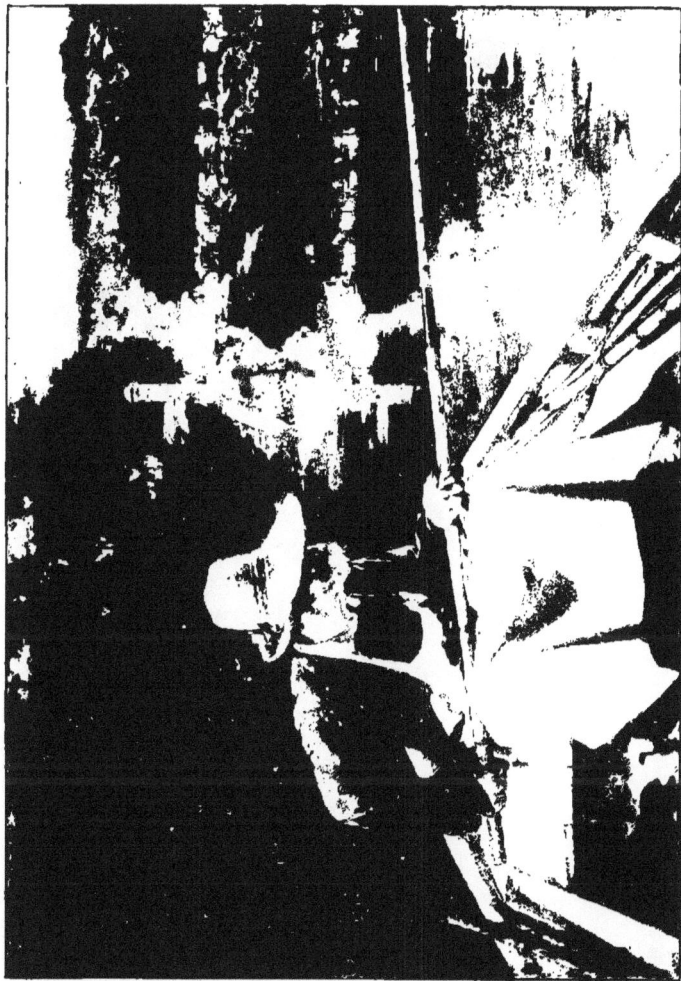

THE ROD

RENÉ GILBERT (France)

ON THE BEACH AT SCHEVENINGEN

H. W. MESDAG (Holland)

A GREEDY GIRL

J. S. H. KEVER (Holland)

IN THE VICINITY OF THE WOLF

OTTO VON THOREN (Austria)

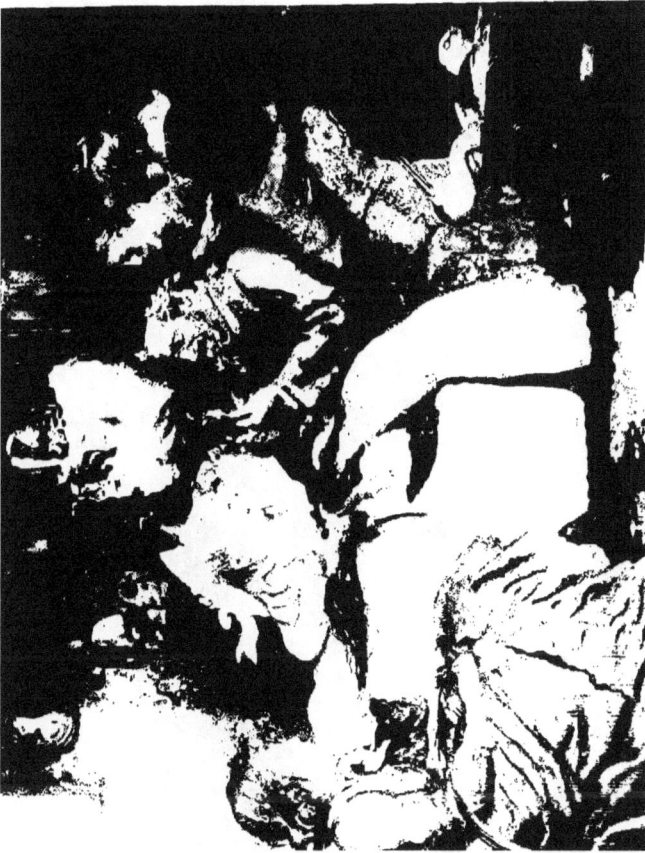

DUSK

WALTER LEISTIKOW (Germany)

MID-DAY LUNCH

M. PEÑA-MUÑOZ (Spain)

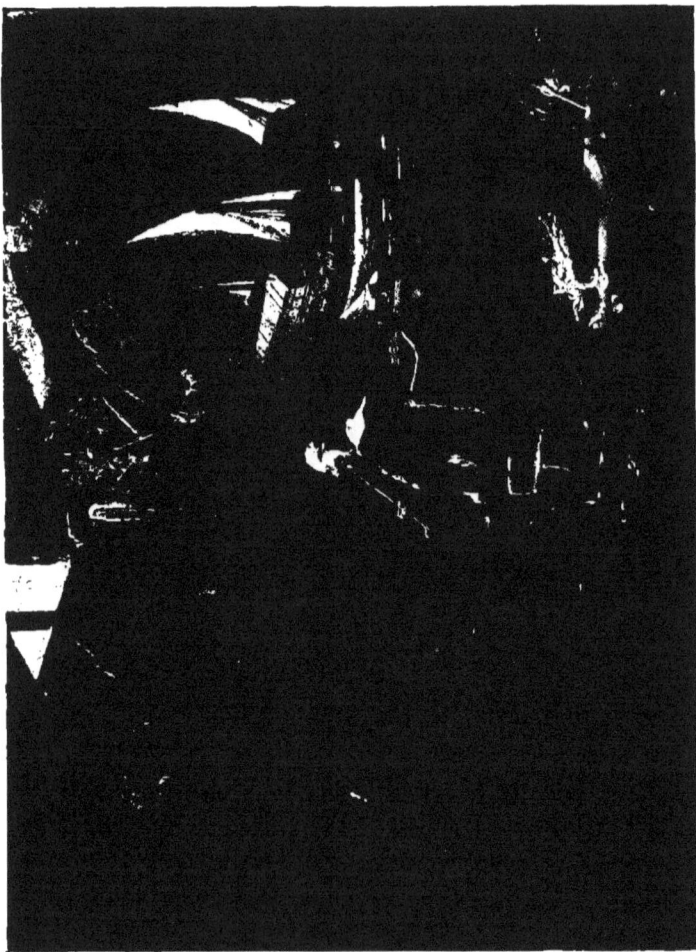

THE FISHERMAN'S HOME

ALFONS SPRING (Germany)

THE HUNT BALL.

JULES L. STEWART (United States)

H. O. WALKER (United States)   THE GIFT-BEARER

L. PASTERNAC (Russia)   RETURNING HOME

R. LEHMANN (Great Britain)   UNDINE

WALTER LANGLEY (Great Britain)   DISASTER

T. OFFERMANS (Holland)   THE VILLAGE CARPENTER

Miss Laura ALMA-TADEMA (Great Britain)   FIRESIDE FANCIES

C. W. BARTLETT (Great Britain)   AN INCIDENT IN THE LIFE OF
                                   THE DAUPHIN

S. E. WALLER (Great Britain)   THE EMPTY SADDLE

IRVING R. WILES (United States) SONATA

A. H. BRAMTOT (France)   FIRST COMMUNION

W. M. CHASE (United States)   ALICE

CHRISTIAN LUDWIG BOCKELMANN (Germany)   A VILLAGE FIRE

WILHELM VOLZ (Germany)   MARIA

T. C. GOTCH (Great Britain)   MY CROWN AND SCEPTRE

D. A. C. ARTZ (Holland)   FALL IN THE FIELDS

ALESANDRO RIQUEA (Italy)   THE DIVINE SHEPHERDESS

F. H. KARL VON UHDE (Germany)   THE ANNOUNCEMENT TO THE SHEPHERDS

CARL VON STETTEN (Germany)   ITALIANS IN PARIS

Hans HERMANN (Germany)   FISHMARKET IN AMSTERDAM

G. L. BULLEID (Great Britain)   A CUSTODIAN

A. P. M. DE RICHEMONT (France)   SACRIFICE

ALBERT MAIGNAN (France)   THE CHAMBER OF THE SIREN

A. F. GORGUET (France)   CONTEMPLATION

OLD CLOTHES MARKET AT THE TEMPLE, PARIS

L. JIMENEZ-ARANDA (Spain)

THE MOWERS' BREAKFAST

E. HENSELER (Germany)

HOLY FAMILY

F. V. Du MOND (United States)

WHO WILL BE CHEATED?

José JIMÉNEZ ARANDA (Spain)

THE CONVENT GARDEN

F. S. WALKER (Great Britain)

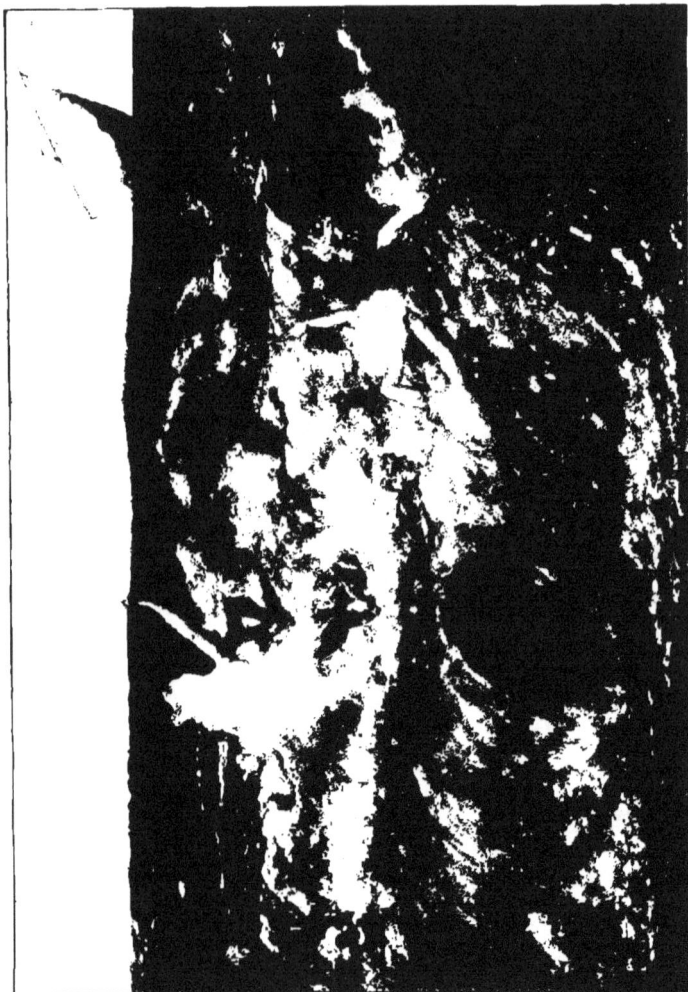

SIRENS

GEO. W. MAYNARD (United States)

DORDRECHT—SUN EFFECT

JACOB MARIS (Holland)

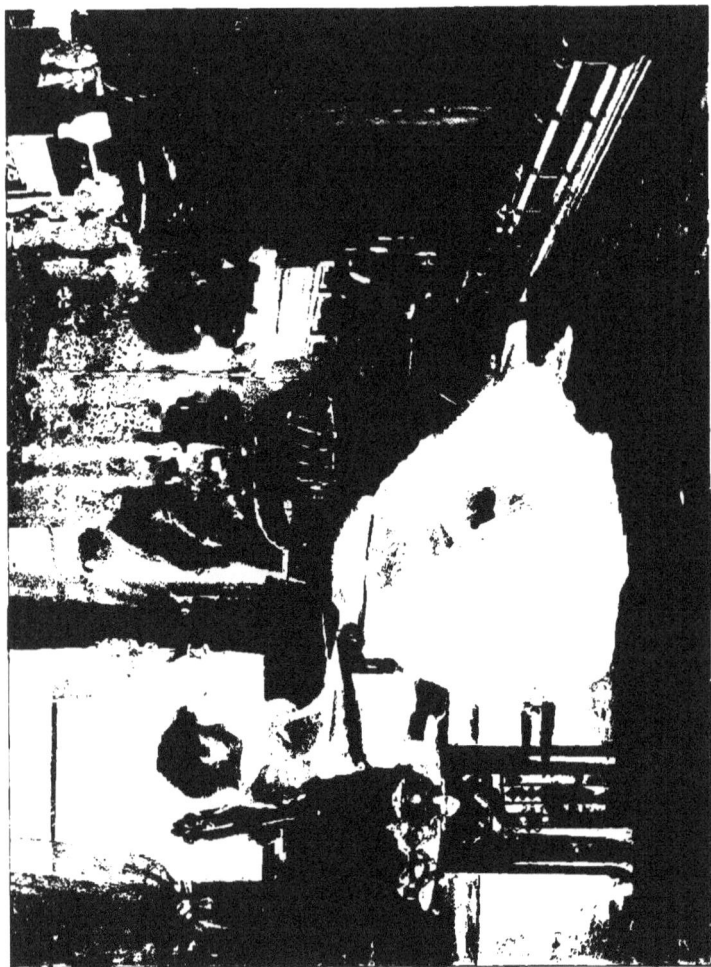

"WOMAN IN YOUR HOURS OF EASE."

C. A. SMITH (Great Britain)

DUTCH CAVALRY

G. H. BREITNER (Holland)

WOOD-CARTS ON THE HEATH

A. MAUVE (Holland)

PARTY ON NUPTIAL EVE IN HOUSE OF THE BRIDE

ALEXIS KORSUKHIN (Russia)

THE MOSCOW RAG-FAIR

VLADIMIR MAKOVSKY (Russia)

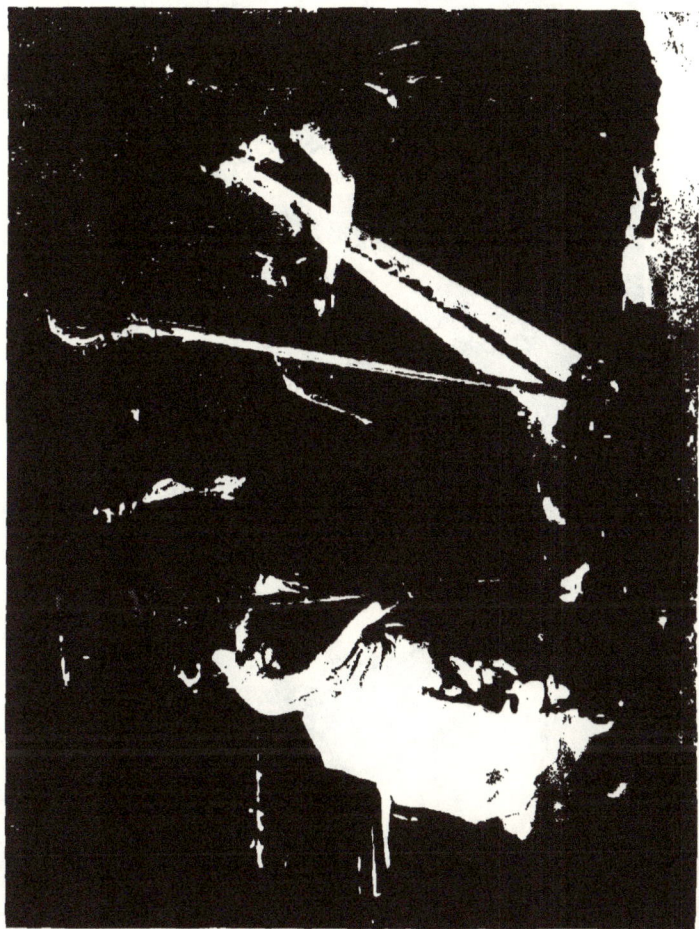

THE TRIO

HERBERT DENMAN (United States)

ALFRED GUILLON (France)   THE LITTLE BROTHER

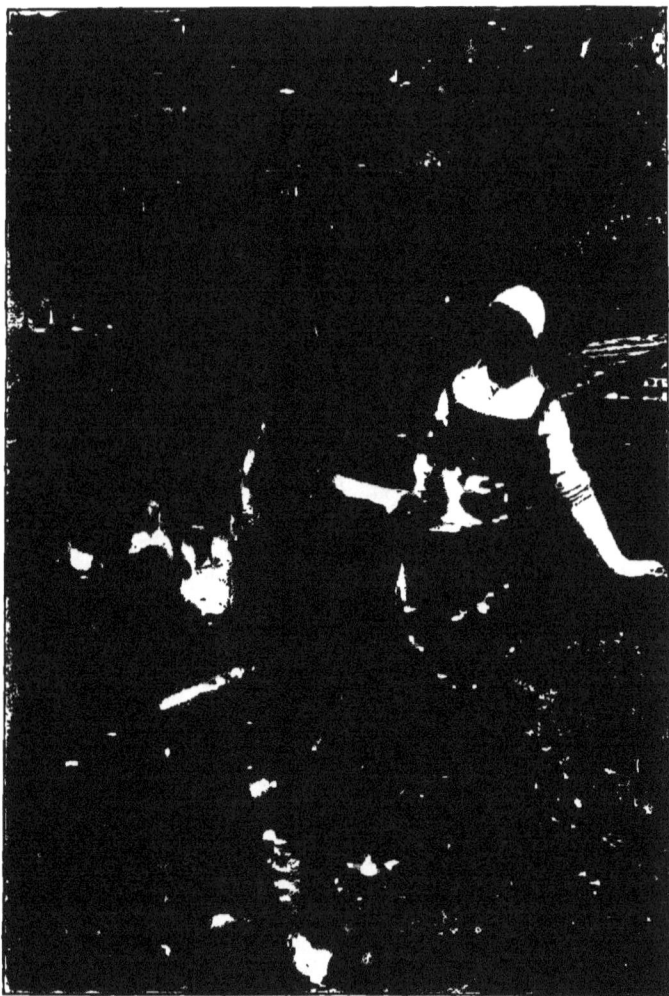

L. JIMENEZ ARANDA (Spain)   THE LOVERS

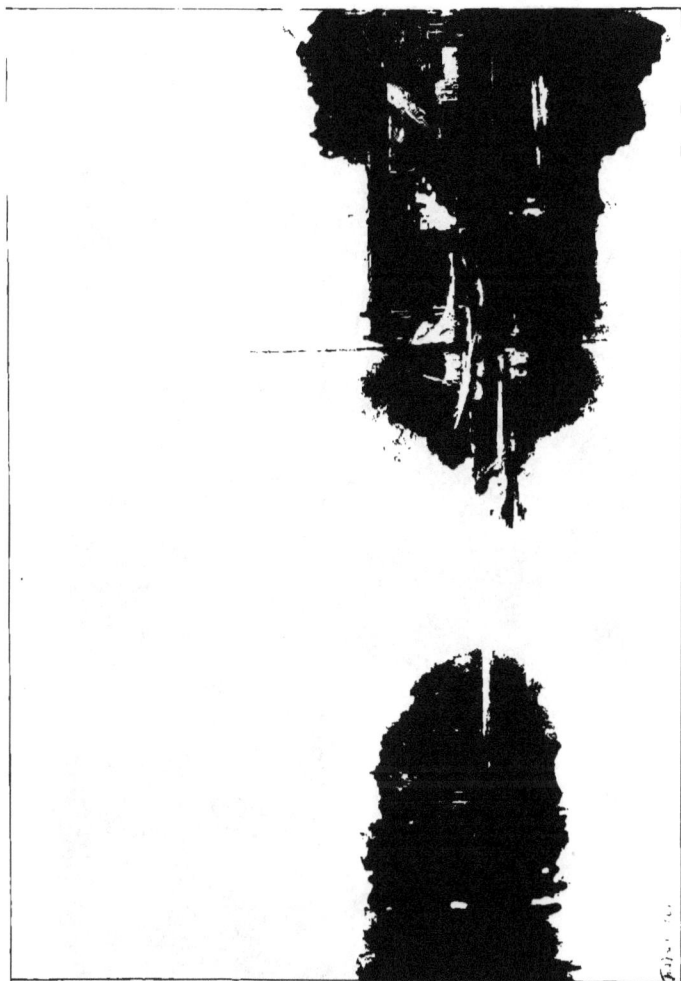

ON THE RIVER VECHT

F. J. DU CHATTEL. (Holland)

EARLY SPRING

ROBT. RUSS (Austria)

THE SIESTA

A. DURST (France)

IN THE LAGOON

RICHARD FRIESE (Germany)

PLOUGHING

ANTON MAUVE (Holland)

RETURN OF THE GRAPE-PICKERS

L. E. ADAN (France)

SHRIMPING AT SCHEVENINGEN

B. J. BLOMMERS (Holland)

NELL AND HER GRANDFATHER

C. GREEN (Great Britain)

E. ROSSET-GRANGER   YOUNG GIRL CHASING BUTTERFLY

THANKSGIVING

AUGUSTO CORRELLI (Italy)

PROTESTANT FUGITIVES—REVOCATION OF EDICT OF NANTES (1685)

MAURICE LELOIR (France)

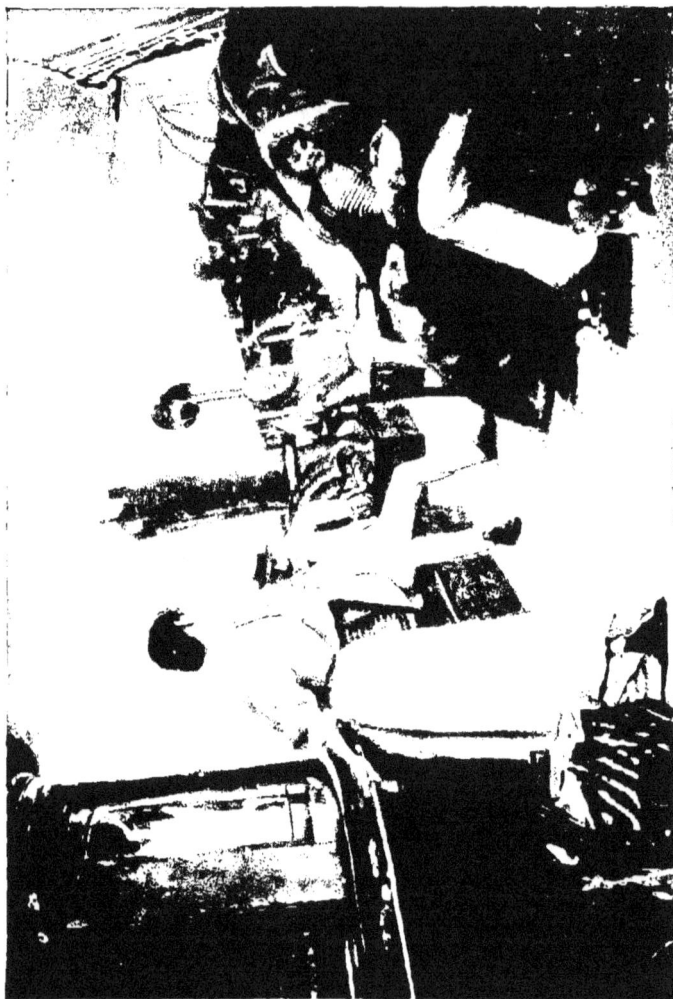

YACHTING

JULES L. STEWART (United States)

"GET UP, DONKEY!"

J. MORENO-CARBONERO (Spain)

THE 9TH OF NOVEMBER—LORD MAYOR'S DAY

W. LOGSDAIL (Great Britain)

RECRUITING FOR SAVONAROLA

F. W. W. TOPHAM (Great Britain)

PAINTING AND POETRY

KENYON COX (United States)

UNDER THE AWNING

J. BERMUDO-MATEOS (Spain)

PEACE

WALTER L. DEAN (United States)

THE FERRY

W. OSBORNE (Great Britain)

SEA URCHINS

R. V. V. SEWELL (United States)

GRAND PRIX DAY

CHILDE HASSAM (United States)

RAFTING ON THE ISAR

KARL KNABL (Germany)

G. E. SENECHAL-DE-HERDRÈVET (France)   RETURN FROM THE OYSTER BEDS AFTER A STORM AT CANCALE

"SUFFER LITTLE CHILDREN TO COME UNTO ME"

JULIUS SCHMID (Austria)

SCOUTS IN FLIGHT

G. GUIGNARD (France)

CONTESTING OWNERSHIP OF THE APPLE OF CONTENTMENT

KARL HARTMANN (Germany)

THE ROLLING-MILL

ERNEST BORDES (France)

BEFORE THE DAYS OF RAPID TRANSIT

E. L. HENRY (United States)

MARKET-DAY, CAIRO

LEOPOLD MÜLLER (Austria)

A SUMMER AFTERNOON

CARL MARR (United States)

DRIVING CATTLE HOMEWARD

J. J. VAN DE SAND BAKHUYZEN (Holland)

CANAL AT AMSTERDAM—SUNSET

K. KLINKENBERG (Holland)

THE ARBITER OF PEACE

N. KOUZNETZOFF (Russia)

IN THE DUNES

TACO MESDAG (Holland)

CHRIST AND THE WOMEN

ALEXANDER D. GOLTZ (Austria)

FOURTH OF JULY PARADE

A. C. HOWLAND (United States)

WYCLIF ON TRIAL

F. MADDOX BROWN ((Great Britain)

A DROWNED MAN

N. DMITRIEV ORENBURGSKY (Russia)

CHRIST AND THE FISHERMEN

F. V. DU MOND (United States)

THE WEDDING-MARCH

AD. HIRSCHEL (Austria)

MONASTIC LIFE

F. V. Du MOND (United States)

PLOUGH BOY

G. CLAUSEN (Great Britain)

A MID-DAY REST

H. FISHER (Great Britain)

Fred. P. VINTON (United States)   PORTRAIT

Anton LAUPHEIMER (Germany)   ST. LUKE

G. F. WATTS (Great Britain)   LOVE AND LIFE

EDMUND C. TARBELL (United States)   GIRL WITH HORSE

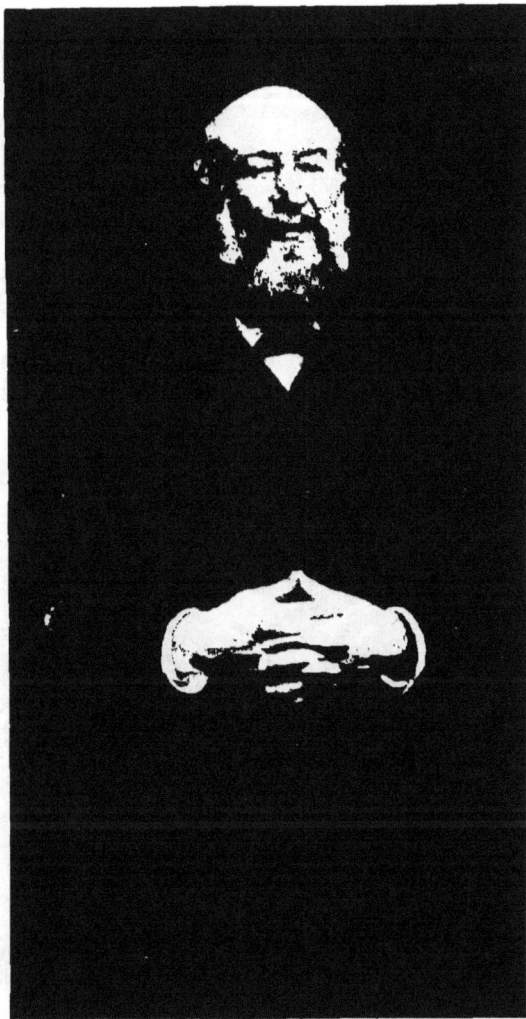

J. CARROLL BECKWITH (United States)   M. ISAACSON

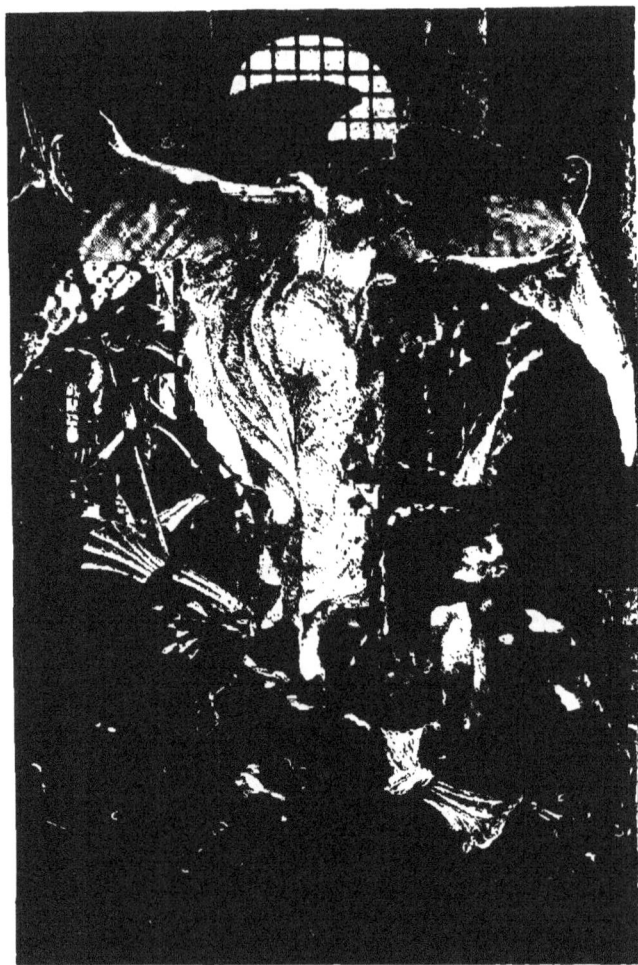

WALTER CRANE (Great Britain)   FREEDOM

JULIA DILLON (United States)   PEONIES

W. ROELOFS (Holland)   PASTURE NEAR THE DUNES

NICHOLAS SAGORSKI (Russia)   HEART-BROKEN BY GRIEF

FRED. W. FREER (United States)   A LADY IN BLACK

I. M. GAUGENGIGL (United States)   THE HAT

AND. L. ZORN (Sweden)   IN THE OMNIBUS

J. DE VRIENDT (Belgium)   A POTTERY SHOP, CAIRO

P. FRANCES Y PASCUAL (Spain)   FATHER'S ADVICE

L. TYTGADT (Belgium)   A LESSON IN EMBROIDERY

R. GORDON HARDIE (United States)   PORTRAIT OF
MRS. HARDIE

"WILL YOU GIVE ME A FLOWER?"

H. VALKENBURG (Holland)

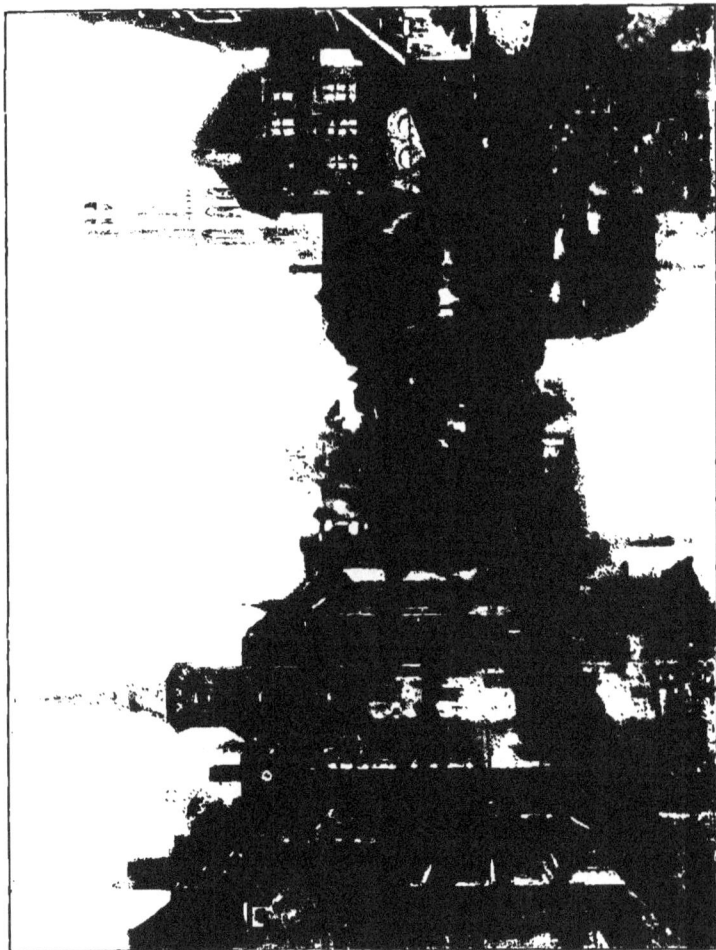

THE OLD CANAL, BRUGES

F. STROOBANT (Belgium)

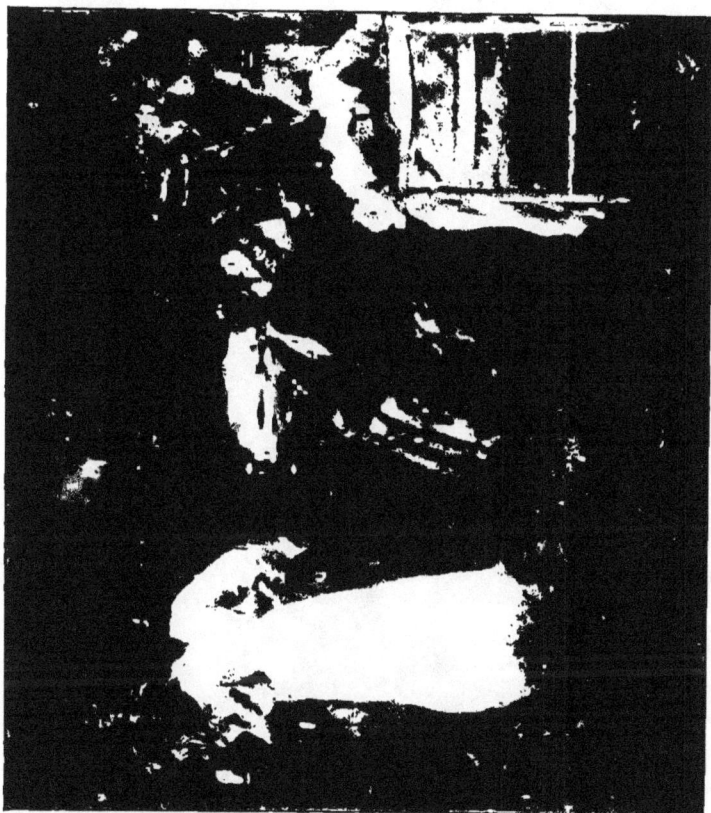

EDMUND C. TARBELL (United States)   IN THE ORCHARD

HOLY WEEK PROCESSION AT SEVILLE

N. DE KEYSER (Belgium)

C. ALVAREZ-DUMONT (Spain)

EPISODE IN THE WAR OF INDEPENDENCE

MILLS NEAR ROTTERDAM

W. ROELOFS (Holland)

CHARLES THE SIXTH

A. DE VRIENDT (Belgium)

THE WATERING-PLACE MARTYRS

JAN VERHAS (Belgium)

EMIGRANTS EMBARKING AT ANTWERP

E. FARASYN (Belgium)

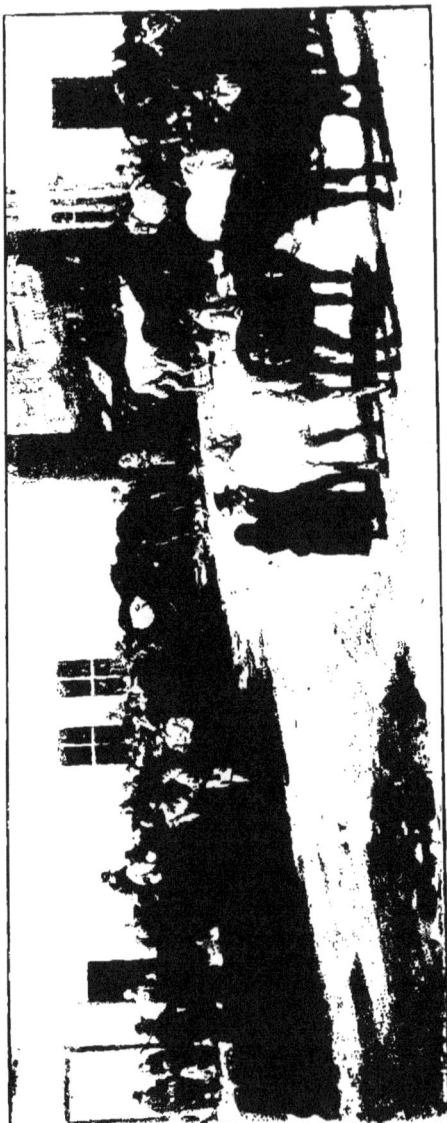

HORSE FAIR AT TONGRES

C. TSCHAGGENY (Belgium)

MUSHROOM GATHERERS

VASSILI GOLYNSKI (Russia)

THE FLAGELLANTS

CARL MARR (United States)

OLIVER TWIST WALKS TO LONDON

JAMES SANT (Great Britain)

COAST OF NORMANDY

MORERA Y GALICIA (Spain)

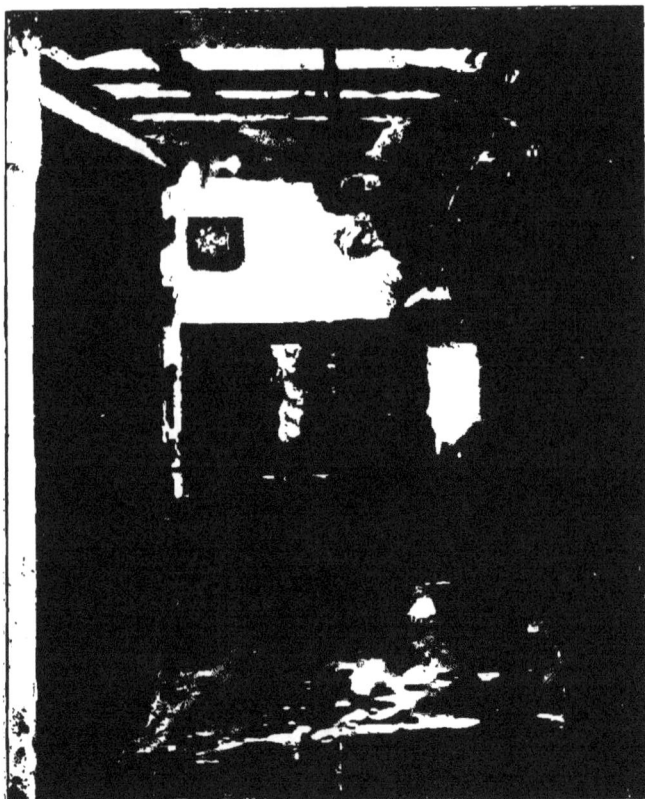

LACE MAKERS

J. VAN SNICK (Belgium)

MISS LAURA ALMA-TADEMA (Great Britain)   BATTLEDORE AND
SHUTTLECOCK

INDEX OF THE ILLUSTRATIONS

—————

353

ARTZ, David Adolf Constant—(𝔥𝔬𝔩𝔩𝔞𝔫𝔡)—*died 1890.*

Born at The Hague, Holland. Pupil of Mollinger and of Josef Israels. Vice-President of the International Jury, Exposition-Universelle, Paris, 1889. Legion of Honor, France, 1889. Member of the French Societe Nationale des Beaux-Arts.

FALL IN THE FIELDS . . . . Page 243

AUBLET, Albert—(𝔣𝔯𝔞𝔫𝔠𝔢)—*75 Boulevard Bineau, Neuilly, Seine.*

Born at Paris. Pupil of J. L. Gerome. Medals, Paris: 3d-class, 1880; Gold Medal, 1889 (Exposition-Universelle). Legion of Honor, 1890.

OLD SAILORS, TRÉPORT . . . . Page 306

BAKHUYZEN VAN DE SAND, Julius Jacobus—(𝔥𝔬𝔩𝔩𝔞𝔫𝔡)— *142 Nieuwe Haven, The Hague.*

Born at The Hague. Pupil of his father. Medals: Vienna, Philadelphia (Centennial Exhibition), 1876, Amsterdam, The Hague and Paris; Silver Medal, Exposition-Universelle, Paris, 1889.

DRIVING HOME THE CATTLE . . . . Page 304

BARILLOT, Léon—(𝔣𝔯𝔞𝔫𝔠𝔢)—*16 rue de la Tour d'Auvergne, Paris.*

Born at Montigny-les-Metz, Lorraine. Pupil of Bonnat. Medals, Paris: 3d-class, 1880; 2d-class, 1884; Gold Medal (Exposition-Universelle), 1889.

THE VALLEY OF THE SEULLES . . . . Page 42
TRAIN 47 . . . . "   43

BARTELS, Hans von—(𝔊𝔢𝔯𝔪𝔞𝔫𝔫)—*Munich.*

Born at Munich. Medal, Paris, 3d-class, 1889.

SURF . . . . Page 47

BARTHOLOME—(𝔣𝔯𝔞𝔫𝔠𝔢).

PASSING THE RING . . . . : . Page 28

BARTLETT, C. W.—(𝔊𝔯𝔢𝔞𝔱 𝔅𝔯𝔦𝔱𝔞𝔦𝔫)—*11 Holland Park Road, W. London.*

AN INCIDENT IN THE LIFE OF THE DAUPHIN . . . Page 233

BARUCCI, Pietro—(𝔍𝔱𝔞𝔩𝔶)—*Rome.*

LAKE IN THE APENNINES . . . . Page 91

BASTERT, Nicholas—(𝔥𝔬𝔩𝔩𝔞𝔫𝔡)—*452 Parkstraat, Amsterdam.*

Bronze Medal, Exposition-Universelle, Paris, 1889.

THE WHITE SAIL . . . . Page 97

BATTAGLIA, Alessandro—(𝔍𝔱𝔞𝔩𝔶)—*5 via Margutta, Rome.*

THE GLEANERS . . . . Page 100

BLOMMERS, Bernardus Johannes—(𝕳𝖔𝖑𝖑𝖆𝖓𝖉)—*17 van Stolkweg, Scheveningen.*
Bronze Medal, Exposition-Universelle, Paris, 1889.

AT BREAKFAST . . . . Page 265
SHRIMPING AT SCHEVENINGEN . . . . "   280
WASHING-DAY . . . . "   94

BOCKELMANN, Christian Ludwig — (𝕲𝖊𝖗𝖒𝖆𝖓𝖞) — *2 Marienstrasse, Düsseldorf.*
Born at St. Jurgen, near Bremen. Pupil of his father, of the Academy at Dusseldorf and of W. Sohn. Medal, Vienna, 1873.

A VILLAGE FIRE . . . . Page 238

BOKS, Evert Jan—(𝕳𝖔𝖑𝖑𝖆𝖓𝖉)—*93 Provinciestraat, Zuid, Antwerp.*
Honorable Mention, Exposition-Universelle, Paris, 1889.

SURPRISED . . . . Page 88

BOMPARD, Maurice—(𝕱𝖗𝖆𝖓𝖈𝖊)—*10 rue Méchain, Paris.*
Born at Rodez. Pupil of G. Boulanger and of J. Lefebvre. 3d-class Medal, Paris, 1880; Bourse-de-voyage, 1882; Silver Medal, Exposition-Universelle, 1889; 2d-class Medal, Paris, 1890.

THE OLD CHELMA GATE . . . . Page 205

BOMPIANI, Angelo—(𝕴𝖙𝖆𝖑𝖞)—*504 Corso, Rome.*

IN THE WOODS . . . . Page 81

BONNEFOY, Henry—(𝕱𝖗𝖆𝖓𝖈𝖊)—*42 rue Fontaine, Paris.*
Born at Boulogne-sur-Mer (Pas de Calais). Pupil of L. Cogniet. Medals, Paris: 3d-class, 1880; 2d-class, 1884. Silver Medal, Exposition-Universelle, Paris, 1889.

A FAMILY . . . . Page 44

BORDES, Ernest—(𝕱𝖗𝖆𝖓𝖈𝖊)—*87 rue Ampère, Paris.*
Born at Pau. Pupil of Bonnat and of Cormon. Honorable Mention, Paris, 1881; Medals: 3d-class, 1884; 2d-class, 1886; Silver Medal, Exposition-Universelle, Paris, 1889.

THE ROLLING-MILL . . . . Page 300

BOURDILLON, Frank N.—(𝕲𝖗𝖊𝖆𝖙 𝕭𝖗𝖎𝖙𝖆𝖎𝖓)—*Dorking, England.*

ON BOARD THE "REVENGE," 1591 . . . . Page 268

BRAMTOT, Alfred Henri—(𝕱𝖗𝖆𝖓𝖈𝖊)—*6 rue du Val-de-Grace, Paris.*
Born at Paris. Pupil of W. A. Bouguereau. 3d-class Medal, Paris, 1879: Prix de Rome, 1879; 2d-class Medal, 1885.

FIRST COMMUNION . . . . Page 236

CHASE, William M.—(**United States**)—*51 West Tenth Street, New York.*

Born in Franklin, Indiana. Pupil of the National Academy and J. O. Eaton, New York, and of the Munich Academy under Piloty. Medals, Munich, 1883; Honorable Mention, Paris, 1881; Silver Medal, 1889 (Exposition-Universelle). Member of the National Academy, New York. President of the Society of American Artists.

ALICE	Page 237
PORTRAIT OF MISS M——	" 231
LAKE SIDE	" 103

DU CHATTEL, Frederick Jacobus—(**Holland**)—*20 Huygenstraat, The Hague.*

ON THE RIVER VECHT	Page 274

CHIGOT, Eugène H. A.—(**France**)—*1 rue des Petitscailloux, rue de l'Eglise et à Valenciennes, Etaples, France.*

Born at Valenciennes. Pupil of Bonnat and Vayson. Honorable Mention, Paris, 1886; 3d-class Medal, 1887; Bourse-de-voyage, 1887; Bronze Medal, Exposition-Universelle, 1889; 2d-class Medal, 1890.

AT ETAPLES—PAS DE CALAIS	Page 192

CLAUSEN, G.—(**Great Britain**)—*Cookham Dean, Berks.*

Silver Medal, Exposition-Universelle, Paris, 1889.

PLOUGH BOY	Page 318

CORELLI, Augusto—(**Italy**)—*Rome.*

THE SERENADE	Page 63
IN THE WOODS	" 225
THANKSGIVING	" 283

CORTESE, Federico—(**Italy**) *21 Via San Paolo, Naples.*

PÆSTUM	Page 139

COURTOIS, Gustave—(**France**)—*73 Boulevard Bineau, Parc de Neuilly, Seine, Paris.*

Born at Pusey (Haute Saone). Pupil of J. L. Gerome. Medals, Paris: 3d-class, 1878; 2d-class, 1880; Gold Medal, Exposition-Universelle, 1889. Legion of Honor, 1889.

PORTRAIT OF MME. GAUTREAU	Page 165

COUTURIER, Léon—(**France**)—*31 Boulevard Berthier, Paris.*

Born at Macon. Pupil of Cabanel and of Danguin. Medal, 3d-class, Paris, 1881; Bronze Medal, 1889 (Exposition-Universelle).

AT THE CAPSTAN—ALL TOGETHER	Page 180

COX, Kenyon—(**United States**)—*145 West Fifty-fifth street, New York.*

Born at Warren, Ohio. Pupil of the Pennsylvania Academy of Fine Arts, Philadelphia, and of Carolus Duran and J. L. Gerome, Paris. Bronze Medal, Salon, Paris, 1889 (Exposition-

DEAN, Walter L.—(**United States**)—*2 Pemberton Square, Boston, Massachusetts.*

DEFREGGER, Franz Ritter—(**Germany**)—*31 König-strasse, Munich, Bavaria.*

Born at Stronach, Austria. Pupil of the Bavarian Royal Academy. 3d-class Medal, Paris, 1878; Medal, Vienna, 1882; Great Gold Medal, Munich. Honorary Member of the Berlin, Vienna and Munich Academies.

DE HAAS, J. H. L.—(**Holland**)—*9 Place de Luxembourg, Brussels, Belgium.*

Born in Hedel, North Brabant. Pupil of Van Oos. Gold Medal, Munich, 1869. Chevalier of the Order of Leopold.

DE KEYSER, Nicaise—(**Belgium**)—*15 rue de la Pépinière, Antwerp.*

Born at Šantvliet. Pupil of Joseph Jacops and of the Royal Academy of Antwerp. Great Gold Medal, Brussels, 1836; 2d-class Medal, Paris, 1840. Order of Leopold, 1839; Officer of the same, 1855. Order of St. Michael of Bavaria, 1851. Order of the Lion, 1844. Legion of Honor, France, 1862.

DELOBBE, François Alfred—(**France**)—*27 rue d'Alésia, Paris.*

Born at Paris. Pupil of Lucas and of Bouguereau. Medals, Paris: 3d-class, 1874; 2d-class, 1875.

DELORT, Charles Edouard—(**France**)—*31 Boulevard Berthier, Paris.*

Born at Nimes. Pupil of Gleyre and of Gerome. Medals, Paris: 3d-class, 1875; 2d-class, 1882. Legion of Honor, 1889.

DEMONT, Adrien-Louis—(**France**)—*Montgeron (Seine-et-Oise).*

Born at Douai (Nord). Pupil of Emile Breton. Medals, Paris: 3d-class, 1879; 2d-class, 1882; Gold Medal, 1889 (Exposition-Universelle). Legion of Honor, 1891.

DEMONT-BRETON, Madame Virginie E.—(**France**)—*Montgeron (Seine-et-Oise).*

Born at Courrieres (Pas de Calais). Pupil of her father, Jules Breton. Medals, Paris; 3d-class, 1881; 2d-class, 1883. Gold Medal, 1889 (Exposition-Universelle).

DURST, Auguste—(**France**)—*51 Avenue de la Défense, Puteaux, Seine, Paris.*
Born at Paris. Pupil of Hebert and of Bonnat. Medal, 2d-class, 1884; Silver Medal, 1889 (Exposition-Universelle).

DUVERGER, Théophile E.—(**France**)—*Ecouen (Seine-et-Oise).*
Born at Bordeaux. Medals, Paris: 3d-class, 1861; Medal, 1865; Bronze Medal, 1889 (Exposition-Universelle).

ENNEKING, John J.—(**United States**)—*174 Tremont street, Boston, Massachusetts.*
Born at Minster, Ohio. Pupil of Bonnat, Paris, and of the Bavarian Royal Academy, Munich.

ERELMAN, Otto—(**Holland**).

FARASYN, Edgard—(**Belgium**)—*2 rue Schul, Antwerp.*
Medals: Sydney, 1879; Melbourne, 1880. Bronze Medal, Exposition-Universelle, 1889.

FISHER, H.—(**Great Britain**)—*Elmfield, Herne Hill, England.*

FISHER, S. M.—(**Great Britain**)—*3575 Campo del Cristo S. Angelo, Venice.*

FLETCHER, B.—(**Great Britain**)—*Esmond, Old Park Road, Enfield, England.*

FRANCES Y PASCUAL, Placido—(**Spain**)—*18 Calle Atocha, Madrid.*
Born at Alcoy. 3d-class Medals, Spanish National Exhibitions of 1871 and 1890.

FREER, Frederick W.—(**United States**)—*Chicago.*
Born at Chicago, Illinois. Pupil of the Bavarian Royal Academy, Munich. Associate of the National Academy, New York.

GOLTZ, Alexander D.—(**Austria**)—*24 Starhemberggasse, Vienna.*
Born at Puspoek-Ladany, Hungary.
CHRIST AND THE WOMEN . . . . Page 311

GOLYNSKI, Vassilli—(**Russia**).
MUSHROOM GATHERERS . . . . Page 346

GORGUET, Auguste François—(**France**)—*6 rue Boissonade, Paris.*
Born at Paris. Pupil of Boulanger, Gerome, Bonnat and Morot. Honorable Mention, 1889, at the Salon and at the Exposition-Universelle.
CONTEMPLATION . . . . Page 255

GOTCH, T. C.—(**Great Britain**)—*The Malt House, Newlyn, Penzance.*
MY CROWN AND SCEPTRE . . . . Page 242

GRAFLY, Charles—(**United States**).
DÆDALUS . . . . Page 85

GREEN, C.—(**Great Britain**)—*20 Shrewsbury road, Sheffield, England.*
THE PICKWICK CLUB . . . . Page 140
NELL AND HER GRANDFATHER . . . . " 281
(Old Curiosity Shop.—DICKENS.)

GUARDA-CASSI, G.—(**Italy**).
THE MAYOR'S WEDDING . . . . Page 82

GUERRA, Achille—(**Italy**).
CIOCARA WITH FLOWERS . . . . Page 84
THE FORTUNE TELLER . . . . " 24

GUIGNARD, Gaston—(**France**).
Born at Bordeaux. Pupil of Humbert, Gervex and Ferry. Medals, Paris: 3d-class, 1884; 2d-class, 1887. Silver Medal, Exposition-Universelle, 1889. Legion of Honor, 1891.
SCOUTS IN FLIGHT . . . . Page 298

GUILLEN-PEDEMONTE, H.—(**Spain**)—*Alicante.*
Born at Alicante. Pupil of Casto Plasencia.
THE LAST BREATH . . . . Page 198

GUILLOU, Alfred—(**France**)—*161 Boulevard Montparnasse, Paris.*
Born at Concarreau (Finistere). Pupil of Cabanel and of Bouguereau. Medals, Paris: 3d-class, 1877; 2d-class, 1881. Silver Medal, 1889 (Exposition-Universelle).
THE LITTLE BROTHER . . . . Page 272

HENRY, Edward L.—(**United States**)—*37 West Fourteenth street, New York.*

Born at Charleston, South Carolina. Pupil of the Pennsylvania Academy of the Fine Arts and of P. Weber, Philadelphia, and of Suisse and Courbet, Paris. Honorable Mention, Exposition-Universelle, Paris, 1889. Member of the National Academy of Design, New York.

BEFORE THE DAYS OF RAPID TRANSIT . . . . . . Page 301
THE WEDDING DAY . . . . " 177

HENSELER, E.—(**Germany**).

HARVESTERS HOMEWARD BOUND . . . . Page 215
THE MOWERS' BREAKFAST . . . . " 257

HERMANN, Hans—(**Germany**)—*82 Steglitzer-strasse, Berlin.*

Silver Medal, Exposition-Universelle, Paris, 1889.

FISH-MARKET IN AMSTERDAM . . . . Page 251

HIRSCHEL, Adolphe — (**Austria**) — *114 Mariahilfer-strasse, Vienna.*

Silver Medal, Exposition-Universelle, Paris, 1889.

THE WEDDING MARCH . . . . Page 316

HOECKER, Paul — (**Germany**) — *24 Nymphenburger-strasse, Munich.*

Bronze Medal, Exposition-Universelle, Paris, 1889.

ON BOARD H. M. S. "DEUTSCHLAND" . . . . . Page 194

HOELZEL, Adolf—(**Germany**)—*Dachau, near Munich, Bavaria.*

LIGHT . . . . Page 116

HOLMAN, Frank S.—(**United States**).

MELODY . . . . Page 22

HOWE, William Henry—(**United States**)—*11 rue Mont-Doré, Paris.*

Born at Ravenna, Ohio. Pupil of de Thoren and Vuillefroy. Honorable Mention, Salon, Paris, 1886; 3d-class Medal, 1888; Silver Medal, Exposition-Universelle, 1889.

NORMAN BULL . . . . Page 50

HOWLAND, Alfred C.—(**United States**)—*52 East Twenty-third street, New York.*

Born at Walpole, New Hampshire. Pupil of the Dusseldorf Academy, and Flamm, Dusseldorf, and of Lambinet, Paris. Member of the National Academy of Design, New York.

FOURTH OF JULY PARADE . . . . Page 312

LUMINAIS, Evariste Vital—(𝔉𝔯𝔞𝔫𝔠𝔢)—*23 rue de la Faisanderie, Paris.*

Born at Nantes. Pupil of Cogniet and Troyon. Medals, Paris: 3d-class, 1852 and 1855 (Exposition-Universelle); Gold Medal, 1889 (Exposition-Universelle). Legion of Honor, 1869.

McILHENNY, C. M.—(𝖀𝖓𝖎𝖙𝖊𝖉 𝕾𝖙𝖆𝖙𝖊𝖘)—*896 Broadway, New York.*

Born at Philadelphia. Member of the American Water Color Society.

Mac EWEN, Walter—(𝖀𝖓𝖎𝖙𝖊𝖉 𝕾𝖙𝖆𝖙𝖊𝖘)—*11 Place Pigalle, Paris.*

Born at Chicago, Illinois. Pupil of Cormon, Paris. Honorable Mention, Salon, Paris, 1886; Silver Medal, Exposition-Universelle, 1889.

MAIGNAN, Albert—(𝔉𝔯𝔞𝔫𝔠𝔢)—*1 rue la Brüyère, Paris.*

Born at Beaumont (Sarthe). Pupil of Luminais. Medals, Paris: 3d-class, 1874; 2d-class, 1876; 1st-class, 1879. Legion of Honor, 1883.

MAKOVSKY, VLADIMIR—(𝕽𝖚𝖘𝖘𝖎𝖆)—*Academy of Fine Arts, Moscow.*

MARAIS, Adolphe Charles—(𝔉𝔯𝔞𝔫𝔠𝔢)—*Honfleur, Calvados.*

Born at Honfleur, Calvados. Pupil of Berchere and of Busson. Medals, Paris: 3d-class, 1880; 2d-class, 1883; Bronze Medal, Exposition, Paris, 1889.

MARIS, Jacob—(𝕳𝖔𝖑𝖑𝖆𝖓𝖉)—*82 Laan van Meerdervoort, The Hague, Holland.*

Born at the Hague. Pupil of The Hague Academy, Strobel and Hebertus Van Hove, of The Hague; of De Keyser and Van Lerias, Antwerp, and of Hebert, Paris. Honorable Mention, Salon, Paris, 1884; Gold Medal, Exposition-Universelle, 1889.

MARR, Carl—(𝖀𝖓𝖎𝖙𝖊𝖉 𝕾𝖙𝖆𝖙𝖊𝖘)—*13 Kaulbach-strasse, Munich, Bavaria.*

Born at Milwaukee, Wisconsin. Pupil of his father and of the Bavarian Royal Academy, Munich. Gold Medal, Prize Fund Exhibition, New York, 1886.

of the Institute of France, 1883. Member of the Academies of Edinburgh, Antwerp, Madrid and Rome.

MOREAU-DE-TOURS, Georges—(𝔉𝔯𝔞𝔫𝔠𝔢)—*51 rue Claude Bernard, Paris.*

Born at Ivry (Seine). Pupil of Cabanel and of Marquerie. Medals, 1864, 1865 and 1869; 2d-class Medal, 1878 (Exposition-Universelle). Legion of Honor, 1875 ; Officer of the Legion, 1883. Member of the Institute of France, 1889.

MORENO-CARBONERO, Jose—(𝔖𝔭𝔞𝔦𝔫).

Born at Malaga. Pupil of Bernardo Ferrandez. 1st-class Medals in the Spanish National Exhibitions of 1881 and 1884. Gold Medals in Exhibitions at Munich, Vienna and Rome. Silver Medal, Exposition-Universelle, Paris, 1889. Grand Gold Medal at Budapesth, 1890. Diploma of Honor, Berlin, 1891.

(From " El Sombrero de tres picos," by Don Pedro A. Alarcon.)

MORERA Y GALICIA, Jaime—(𝔖𝔭𝔞𝔦𝔫)—*65 Calle Atocha, Madrid.*

Pupil of Carlos de Haes. Awarded two 2d-class Medals at Spanish National Exhibitions.

MORRIS, Philip Richard—(𝔊𝔯𝔢𝔞𝔱 𝔅𝔯𝔦𝔱𝔞𝔦𝔫)—*33 St. John's Wood Road, London.*

Born at Devonport, England. Pupil of the Royal Academy Schools and of Holman Hunt. As a student, was awarded Gold Medal and traveling studentship fund. Elected A.R.A., 1887. Medal, 2d-class, Antwerp Exhibition, 1885. Bronze Medal, Exposition-Universelle, Paris, 1889.

MUENIER, Jules Alexis—(𝔉𝔯𝔞𝔫𝔠𝔢).

Born at Vesoul. Medal, 3d-class, 1887 ; Bourse-du-voyage, 1887.

MULLER, Leopold—(𝔄𝔲𝔰𝔱𝔯𝔦𝔞)—*3 Schiller-platz, Vienna.*

Born at Dresden. Pupil of Carl Blaas and Christian Ruben. 1st-class Medal, Munich, 1883. Professor in the Vienna Academy.

MULLER, Peter Paul—(𝔊𝔢𝔯𝔪𝔞𝔫𝔶)—*70 Linprunn-strasse, Munich.*

Bronze Medal, Exposition-Universelle, Paris, 1889.

PALMER, Walter L.—(United States)—*5 Lafayette street, Albany, New York.*

Born at Albany, New York. Pupil of F. E. Church, New York, and of Carolus Duran, Paris. Awarded second Hallgarten Prize, National Academy, New York, 1887. Member of the Society of American Artists. Associate of the National Academy, New York.

EARLY SNOW . . . . Page 191

PARIS, Camille—(France)—*16 rue de Vintimille, Paris.*

Born at Paris. Pupil of Ary Scheffer and of Picot. Medals, Paris: 3d-class, 1874; 2d-class, 1889. Bronze Medal, Exposition-Universelle, 1889.

OLD GATE OF THE TIBER AT ROME . . . . Page 176

PARSONS, Orrin Sheldon—(United States)—*249 West Fourteenth street, New York.*

A LAWN-TENNIS PARTY . . . . Page 185

PASTERNAC, L.—(Russia).

RETURNING HOME . . . . Page 228

PAULI, Georg.—(Sweden)—*11, Fjellgatan, Stockholm.*

Born at Stockholm. Pupil of the Academy of Fine Arts, Stockholm. Honorable Mention, Salon, Paris, 1884. Bronze Medal, Exposition-Universelle, 1889.

A MIDSUMMER NIGHT . . . . Page 65

PEARCE, Charles Sprague—(United States)—*Anvers-sur-Oise (Seine-et-Oise), France.*

Born at Boston, Massachusetts. Pupil of Bonnat, Paris. Honorable Mention, Salon, Paris, 1881; 3d-class Medal, 1883. Member of the International Jury, Exposition-Universelle, Paris, 1889.

THE ANNUNCIATION . . . . Page 204
THE SHEPHERDESS . . . . " 129
MADAM P—— . . . . " 113

PELEVIN, T. A.—(Russia).

THE FIRST BORN . . . . Page 175

PENA-MUNOZ, Maximo—(Spain)—*34 Calle Hortaleza, Madrid.*

Born at Cuenca. Pupil of Casto Plasencia. 3d-class Medal, Spanish National Exhibition, 1887.

MIDDAY LUNCH . . . . Page 222

PENFOLD, Frank C.—(United States)—*Paris, France.*

Born at Lockport, New York.

THE HERRING SEASON . . . . Page 138

PENNACCHINI, Domenico—(Italy)—*Rome.*

Silver Medal, Exposition-Universelle, Paris, 1889.

CRAZY . . . . Page 148

RIQUER, Alejandro—(𝔖𝔭𝔞𝔦𝔫)—*Barcelona.*
Born at Barcelona.
THE DIVINE SHEPHERDESS . . . . Page 244

ROELOFS, Willem—(𝔥𝔬𝔩𝔩𝔞𝔫𝔡)—*20 Rijnstraat, The Hague.*
Silver Medal, Exposition-Universelle, 1889.
MILLS NEAR ROTTERDAM . . . . Page 341
PASTURE NEAR THE DUNES . . . .   "   327

ROSSET-GRANGER, Edouard—(𝔉𝔯𝔞𝔫𝔠𝔢)—*5 rue Martin, Paris.*
Born at Vincennes (Seine). Pupil of Dubufe, Mazarolle and Cabanel. Bourse-de-voyage, 1881; 3d-class Medal, Salon, Paris, 1884; Silver Medal, Exposition-Universelle, 1889.
YOUNG GIRL CHASING A BUTTERFLY . . . . Page 282

ROZIER, Dominique—(𝔉𝔯𝔞𝔫𝔠𝔢)—*34 Boulevard de Clichy, Paris.*
Pupil of Vollon. 3d-class Medal, Salon, Paris, 1876; 2d-class Medal, 1880; Bronze Medal, 1889 (Exposition-Universelle).
FISHMONGERS, DIEPPE . . . . Page 29

RUSS, Robt.—(𝔄𝔲𝔰𝔱𝔯𝔦𝔞)—*3 Münzgasse, Vienna.*
EARLY SPRING . . . . Page 275

SAGORSKI, Nicholas—(𝔚𝔲𝔰𝔰𝔦𝔞).
HEART-BROKEN . . . . Page 328
AT BREAKFAST . . . .   "   131

SAINTIN, Jules Emile—(𝔉𝔯𝔞𝔫𝔠𝔢)—*56 rue du Rocher, Paris.*
Born at Lenie (Aisne). Pupil of Drolling, of Picot and of Laboucher. Medals, Paris, 1866 and 1870. Legion of Honor, 1887. Bronze Medal, Exposition-Universelle, 1889.
REVERIE . . . . Page 112

SANT, James—(𝔊𝔯𝔢𝔞𝔱 𝔅𝔯𝔦𝔱𝔞𝔦𝔫)—*43 Lancaster Gate, Hyde Park, London, England.*
Born at London. Pupil of John Varley and of the Royal Academy. Elected Associate of the Royal Academy, 1861; Royal Academician, 1871. In 1872, appointed Principal Painter in Ordinary to the Queen. Bronze Medal, Exposition-Universelle, 1889.
OLIVER TWIST WALKS TO LONDON . . . . Page 349

SANTORO, Rubens—(𝔍𝔱𝔞𝔩𝔶)—*15 Corso Umberto, Naples.*
NAPLES . . . . Page 134

SCHMID, Julius—(𝔄𝔲𝔰𝔱𝔯𝔦𝔞)—*20 Heugasse, Vienna.*
SUFFER LITTLE CHILDREN TO COME UNTO ME . . Page 297

SCHNARS-ALQUIST, H. — (𝔊𝔢𝔯𝔪𝔞𝔫𝔶) — *82 Lützow-strasse, Berlin.*
Art Commissioner for Germany at the World's Columbian Exposition.
GOING FREELY . . . . Page 182

SINIBALDI, Paul Jean Raphael—(**France**)—*49 Boulevard Mont-parnasse, Paris.*
Born at Paris. Pupil of Alexandre Cabanel and of Alfred Stevens. Honorable Mention, Salon, 1886. Bourse-du-voyage, 1888. Bronze Medal, 1887; Exposition Universelle, 1889.

SMITH, C. A.—(**Great Britain**)—*72 Park Road, Haverstock Hill, London, England.*

SNICK, J. Van—(**Belgium**).

SPRING, Alfons—(**Germany**)—*24 Nymphenburger-strasse, Munich.*
Honorable Mention, Exposition-Universelle, Paris, 1889.

STETTEN, Carl von   (**Germany**).
Born at Augsburg. Pupil of Lefebvre, Boulanger, Courtois and Dagnan-Bouveret. 3d-class Medal, 1884; Bronze Medal, Exposition-Universelle, 1889.

STEWART, Jules L.—(**United States**)—*36 rue Copernic, Paris.*
Born at Philadelphia. Pupil of Zamacois, of Gerome and of Madrazo. Honorable Mention, Salon, Paris, 1885. 3d-class Medal, 1890.

STROOBANT, F.—(**Belgium**)—*20 rue Van Aa, Brussels.*
Born at Brussels. Pupil of Wauters. Medals: Brussels, 1854; London, 1861; Vienna, 1873.

TARBELL, Edmund C.—(**United States**)—*24 Albany street, Dorchester, Massachusetts.*
Born at West Groton, Massachusetts. Pupil of Boulanger and of Lefebvre.

TAYLER, A. Chevalier—(**Great Britain**)—*Newlyn, Penzance.*

TEMPLE, Hans—(**Austria**)—*Belvederegasse, Vienna.*

THOMAS, S. Seymour—(**United States**)—*6 rue de l'Arrivee, Paris.*

Born in Texas. Pupil of Benjamin-Constant, of Lefebvre and of Doucet.

AN INNOCENT VICTIM . . . . Page 38

THOREN, Otto von—(**Austria**)

Born at Vienna. Studied in Brussels and Paris. Medals: Paris, 1865; Munich, 1869; Vienna, 1882. Member of the Order of Francis Joseph and the Russian Order of Vladimir.

IN THE VICINITY OF THE WOLF . . . . Page 219

TIFFANY, Louis C.—(**United States**)—*7 East Seventy-second street, New York.*

Pupil of George Inness and of Samuel Colman, New York, and of Leon Belly, Paris. Member of the National Academy and of the Society of American Artists, New York.

MARKET AT NUREMBERG . . . . Page 348
TAMING THE FLAMINGO . . . . " 115

TIRATELLI, Aurelio—(**Italy**)—*33 via Margutta, Rome.*

COUNTRY LIFE—ROMAN APENNINES . . . . Page 25

TITCOMB, William Holt Yates—(**Great Britain**)—*Ockham House, Culverden Road, London, England.*

Born at Cambridge, England. Pupil of Boulanger, of Lefebvre and of Cormon, Paris. 3d-class Medal, Salon, Paris, 1890.

PRIMITIVE METHODISTS AT ST. IVES, CORNWALL . . Page 76

TOMMASI, Publio de—(**Italy**).

GAME OF CHESS—IN THE VATICAN . . . . Page 121

TOPHAM, Francis W. W.—(**Great Britain**).

Born in London. Pupil of his father, Francis W. Topham, and of the Royal Academy. Member of the British Society of Water-color Painters.

RECRUITING FOR SAVONAROLA . . . . Page 288

TOUDOUZE, Edouard—(**France**)—*21 Boulevard des Batignolles, Paris.*

Born at Paris. Pupil of Pils and of Leloir. Prix de Rome, 1871. 3d-class Medal, Salon, Paris, 1876; 2d-class Medal, 1877; Silver Medal, Exposition-Universelle, 1889. Legion of Honor, 1892.

THE CRADLE . . . . Page 64

TRUESDELL, Gaylord S.—(**United States**)—*Hotel Saint-Malo, 2 rue d' Odessa, Paris.*

Born in the United States. Pupil of A. Morot and of Cormon. Bronze Medal, Exposition-Universelle, Paris, 1889.

THE SHEPHERD AT HIS LUNCH . . . . Page 37

TRUPHEME, Auguste—(**France**)—*23 rue de Sevres, Paris.*
Born at Aix (Bouches-du-Rhone). Pupil of Flandrin, of Cornu, of Henner and of Bouguereau. 3d-class Medal, Salon, Paris, 1884; 2d-class, 1888; Bronze Medal, 1889 (Exposition-Universelle).
SINGING LESSON IN A COMMON SCHOOL IN PARIS . . Page 141

TSCHAGGENY, Charles Philogene — (**Belgium**) — *1 rue de l'Abondance, Brussels.*
Born at Brussels. Pupil of Eugene Verboeckhoven. Medals: Brussels, 1842 and (Gold Medal), 1845; Oporto, 1856; Vienna, 1873; Philadelphia, 1876. Officer of the Order of Leopold, 1875.
HORSE-FAIR AT TONGRES . . . . Page 345

TUKE, Henry Scott—(**Great Britain**)—*Linden Lodge, Hanwell, London.*
Born at York, England. Honorable Mention, Salon, Paris, 1891.
SAILORS PLAYING CARDS . . . . Page 109

TVOROJUIKOF, J. J.—(**Russia**).
GRANDMOTHER AND GRAND-DAUGHTER . . . . . . Page 69

TVOROZHNIKOV, Ivan—(**Russia**).
A LAY BROTHER; IMAGE-SELLER . . . . Page 17

TYTGADT, Louis—(**Belgium**)—*Brussels.*
Born at Lovendegem, Belgium. Honorable Mention, Salon, Paris, 1886. Bronze Medal, Exposition-Universelle, Paris, 1889.
A LESSON IN EMBROIDERY . . . . Page 334

UHDE, Friedrich Hermann Karl von—(**Germany**)—*75 Theresienstrasse, Munich.*
Born at Walkenburg, Saxony. Pupil of M. de Munkacsy, in Paris. 3d-class Medal, Salon, Paris, 1885. Grand Prix, 1889 (Exposition-Universelle). Legion of Honor, 1891. Associate of the French Societe Nationale des Beaux Arts.
THE ANNOUNCEMENT TO THE SHEPHERDS . . . . Page 245

ULRICH, Charles F.—(**United States**)—*Munich.*
Pupil of the National Academy of Design, New York, and of Loefftz and Lindenschmidt, in Munich. Awarded the Clarke Prize, National Academy of Design, New York, 1884; a $2500 cash prize in a prize-fund exhibition held in New York, 1886; Bronze Medal, Exposition-Universelle, Paris, 1889. Member of the Society of American Artists, and Associate of the National Academy, New York.
ITALIAN IDYL . . . . Page 212

VAIL, Eugene—(**United States**)—*27 bis rue Bayen, Paris.*
Born at St. Malo, of American parents. Pupil of the Art Students' League, New York, of l'Ecole des Beaux-Arts, and of Cabanel, Collin and Dagnan-Bouveret, Paris. 3d-class Medal, Salon, Paris, 1888; Gold Medal, Exposition-Universelle, 1889.
MARINE . . . . Page 18

WAHLBERG, Alfred—(𝕾𝖜𝖊𝖉𝖊𝖓)—*157 rue de Rome, Paris.*

Born at Stockholm. Pupil of the School of Fine Arts at Stockholm. Medal, Salon, Paris, 1870; 2d-class Medal, 1872. Legion of Honor, 1874. 1st-class Medal, 1878 (Exposition-Universelle). Officer of the Legion of Honor, 1878.

NIGHT ON THE SWEDISH COAST . . . . Page 93

WALKER, F. S.—(𝕲𝖗𝖊𝖆𝖙 𝕭𝖗𝖎𝖙𝖆𝖎𝖓)—*1 England's Lane, Haverstock Hill, London, England.*

THE CONVENT GARDEN . . . . Page 260

WALKER, Henry Oliver—(𝖀𝖓𝖎𝖙𝖊𝖉 𝕾𝖙𝖆𝖙𝖊𝖘)—*253 West Forty-second street, New York.*

Born in Boston. Pupil of Bonnat, Paris. Member of the Society of American Artists.

THE GIFT-BEARER . . . . Page 227

WALLER, Samuel Edmund—(𝕲𝖗𝖊𝖆𝖙 𝕭𝖗𝖎𝖙𝖆𝖎𝖓)—*12 Girdless Road, West Kensington, London, England.*

Born at Gloucester, England. Pupil of the Gloucester School of Art and. of the Royal Academy.

THE EMPTY SADDLE . . . . Page 234

WALTON, Frank—(𝕲𝖗𝖊𝖆𝖙 𝕭𝖗𝖎𝖙𝖆𝖎𝖓)—*Holmbury, St. Mary, Dorking, England.*

WRECK OF THE SPANISH ARMADA . . . . Page 107

WARD, Mrs. E. M.—(𝕲𝖗𝖊𝖆𝖙 𝕭𝖗𝖎𝖙𝖆𝖎𝖓)—*3 Chester House, Chester Square, S.W., London, England.* (Wife of James Ward, R.A.)

MRS. FRY VISITING NEWGATE . . . . Page 62

WATTS, George Frederick — (𝕲𝖗𝖊𝖆𝖙 𝕭𝖗𝖎𝖙𝖆𝖎𝖓) — *Little Holland House, Kensington, London.*

Born at London. Pupil of the Royal Academy. Awarded prize of £300 in competition for the decoration of the Houses of Parliament (1842) and a prize of £500 for a cartoon in 1847. Elected A.R.A., 1867; R.A., 1868. Medals: 1st-class, Paris, 1878 (Exposition-Universelle). Legion of Honor, 1878. 1st-class Medal, Antwerp, 1885.

LOVE AND LIFE . . . . Page 322

WEEKS, Edward Lord — (𝖀𝖓𝖎𝖙𝖊𝖉 𝕾𝖙𝖆𝖙𝖊𝖘) — *128 Avenue de Wagram.*

Born at Boston, Massachusetts. Pupil of l'Ecole des Beaux-Arts, of Bonnat and of Gerome. Honorable Mention, Salon, Paris, 1884; 3d-class Medal, 1889; Gold Medal, 1889 (Exposition-Universelle).

THE GANGES . . . . Page 154
THREE BEGGARS OF CORDOVA . . . . " 108

www.ingramcontent.com/pod-product-compliance
Lightning Source LLC
Chambersburg PA
CBHW030913270326
41929CB00008B/675